Curiosity Expands Your Mind

Curiosity Expands Your Mind

A Resource Book for Truth Seekers

Brenda Miller
Austin, Texas

Order this book online at www.trafford.com
or email orders@trafford.com

Most Trafford titles are also available at major online book retailers.

Note for Librarians: A cataloguing record for this book is available from Library
and Archives Canada at www.collectionscanada.ca/amicus/index-e.html

Printed in Victoria, BC, Canada.

ISBN: 978-1-4251-8856-6 (Soft)

*We at Trafford believe that it is the responsibility of us all, as both individuals
and corporations, to make choices that are environmentally and socially sound.
You, in turn, are supporting this responsible conduct each time you purchase a
Trafford book, or make use of our publishing services. To find out how you are
helping, please visit www.trafford.com/responsiblepublishing.html*

*Our mission is to efficiently provide the world's finest, most comprehensive
book publishing service, enabling every author to experience success.
To find out how to publish your book, your way, and have it available
worldwide, visit us online at www.trafford.com*

Trafford rev. 7/28/2009

North America & international
toll-free: 1 888 232 4444 (USA & Canada)
phone: 250 383 6864 ♦ fax: 812 355 4082 ♦ email: info@trafford.com

For my guardian angels, my spirit guides, and
my beautiful daughter, Mikayla, for putting up with me.
All my love.

This book started out as my way of trying to make sense of the different religions, why we believe the way we believe, or see the world as we do.

Brought up in the Christian faith, I was told that certain things were the "Devil's work." To become more informed, or to really understand this so called "Devil's work," I had to look at other religions or different belief systems. At first, I was hesitant to begin because of the fears that were instilled into my very essence, my belief system, but I overcame my fears with my need to know, and so began my search for understanding.

My search began in 2003. I joined the Austin Herb Society, which I was elected as editor of their monthly newsletter, *The Potpourri*. I had never been an editor of anything before, so what were they thinking by electing me to such a position. My knowledge of herbs, herbal lore, or anything that would be of use to the Austin Herb Society, was very limited or to be very honest, non-existent. It was an education for me, as the members of the Austin Herb Society are all very knowledgeable and I learned so much from them, a big thank you is being sent out to them right now. Well, like any ill-informed knowledge seeker of the 21st Century, I began with the Internet, and as the saying goes, the rest is history.

It is amazing all the different sites that pop up when you type in "Uses for Basil," etc. Not only did the food references come up, but magical references came up as well. And as you know, I was hesitant to check out such magical uses. But, I did. What is really amazing about my search or research is, that I began to understand my connection with Nature, the Universe, God, Spirit, etc. I am now able to worship or relate to God/Spirit out of love and understanding and not fear or because it is expected out of me. Now, I actually acknowledge my angels, because before now I was taught not do that, it was wrong. I now invite them in each and every day, talk to them, rejoice with them, as I know that they are sent to me from God/Spirit/Source as a gift of unconditional love. I also feel the presence of the fairies, which I like to call "earth angels," as they are in charge of nurturing Mother Earth, and me as well.

It is my hope that you find this book interesting, informative, and insightful. That your curiosity in purchasing this book will cause you to open your mind to other possibilities, to other realms of existence, or worship, to see that we are all one, that it really is a small world. Take this book as a starting point for your search or research in your quest for knowledge and understanding of this world.[1]

Enjoy, and happy discovering.

Brenda Miller
May 2009
Austin, Texas

---

1 This book is for entertainment purposes only and is not to be misconstrued otherwise. ॐ

Table of Contents

AFFIRMATIONS

Affirmations are the positive statements you make to yourself. They are said in times of encouragement to overcome certain fears, or to encourage yourself to make changes in your life. But, you also have statements that you have learned from others that are negative, negative statements about yourself. In order to change these negative statements to positive statements, you need to change that voice in your head to say positive things about yourself. By saying these new statements or affirmations, you will change your sub-conscious mind from negative thoughts of yourself to positive thoughts of yourself. Your sub-conscious mind only repeats what it is told. If your conscious mind says things such as "You can't write a book because you're not smart enough. You don't have the imagination for writing a book, so what makes you think that you can do this?" Or, "You're fat, who would love you?" Or, "You're not worthy, and who would want you to join their activity or club?" You need to change the way that you think about yourself, and by consciously saying positive affirmations to yourself every day, your sub-conscious mind will start saying encouraging statements. It would encourage you to take that writing class at the local community college, or encourage you to get out and meet people, join a club, start an exercise program, etc. Below, you will learn how to construct affirmations, there are a few examples of good positive affirmations that may be used as they are, or modify them to fit your particular circumstance. Take one day at a time and enjoy the blessings that it holds for you. Learn to love and support the beautiful person that you are, start by constructing and saying positive affirmations today.

Constructing affirmations:

- It is best to write the affirmation. The act of writing focuses your attention and clarifies what you are seeking to experience.

- Make it short and concise. It is all right to use affirmations that have been written by others, but writing them out again by hand energizes your sub-conscious. Do not concern yourself with how pretty or poetic the words are.

- The affirmation should be in present tense. *Example:* It is more effective to say, "I am healthy and fit," then to say, "I will become healthy and fit."

- Post your affirmations in several places where you will see them throughout the day: bathroom, car, office/work area, bedroom, etc.

- Repeat the affirmation as often as you can daily. If possible, say it aloud, but saying it silently to yourself will also work. Repeating the affirmation three-times, each time it is said, really makes it sink in.

- If you have difficulty staying with the process, stand in front of a mirror and observe yourself as you speak the affirmation with confidence. Stand tall. Be confident and have enthusiasm while saying the affirmation(s).

- After a while, you may need to re-write your affirmations. As issues are resolved or changed, or you are working on, or focusing on other areas of your life, your affirmations will change as well. Our issues are like the layers of an onion. One layer peels off because it no longer serves us and we are able to move on to another layer to peel off and release.

- In the beginning of your life, your thoughts and beliefs were shaped by your family members. As you grew and developed relationships outside your family, (peers, boyfriends/girlfriends, or spouses/partners) your beliefs and thoughts were formed by these new relationships. Some of these relationships may still be a part of your life, or they may not, but those beliefs/thoughts are still with you. As you are moving and growing towards a more peaceful and spiritual existence, these beliefs or thoughts are no longer acceptable or fit into your new life, and now you need to release them. Affirmations help to erase the old belief patterns that no longer serve you, and/or no longer serve a purpose in your new life.

- Be patient with yourself and love yourself. You are a wonderful and unique being. Do not be too hard on yourself while working with your affirmations. Just take each day, one day at a time. It takes 21 days to retrain your brain and 21 days to make it a habit or to make it stick.

Affirmation examples:

- I am a fully awakened, vital, and spiritual being superior to all circumstances.

- I am made in the image and likeness of God, I have within me everything necessary for my complete expression in life.

- I am open to the flow of Life and I allow it to be expressed freely through me. I give nothing, but God gives everything to me.

- I am beautiful.

- I deserve the best that the Universe has to offer and I deserve it right now.

- I am loved and I am loving.

- I want for nothing, all my needs are met.

- I can do anything that I want to do and I do not need anyone's permission.

- I choose happiness, by acting on my own behalf rather than reacting to others.

- Today is the only place in time that exists. I release my past, and everything, and everyone in it.

- I now release my old belief patterns and let go of all my old, self-defeating habits.

- I let go of all my controlling thoughts and behaviors, and know that God will take care of me.

- Today I will expect all to go well, and everything is in Divine order.

- I release my pain, I am healthy, fit, and full of life.

- I trust that the changes in my life are necessary and good for me.

- I am not a victim.

- I accept my fears and move forward in spite of them.

AMULETS AND/OR TALISMANS

The wearing of amulets (bracelets, necklaces, rings, etc.) originated in the animistic[2] beliefs and practices, which attributed power and influence to the spirit world. These amulets[3] or talismans were worn for protection against bad luck or negative forces. Ears were seen as the means of entry and exit of spirits, and as the seat of intelligence. By wearing gemstone earrings, one would be connecting that particular stone's healing power to one's psyche. Wearing certain perfumes or essential oils served the purpose of attraction or repulsion. Drawings, pictures, statues such as crosses, pictures of Christ, and angels are used in homes and businesses to remind one of God's (the Creator's) presence. Tattoos are also used

---

2 Animism or animistic belief is that all natural objects, such as trees; stones; plants; animals; birds or insects, possess an inherent spiritual being or soul.
3 Amulets are used for attracting or bringing good/positive energy or substance. Talismans are used for protection from bad/negative energy or substance.

as protective amulets. Carrying a rabbit's foot is a good luck charm (amulet). In modern times, we wear these items because they are pretty or make us feel pretty. Tattoos are used as a way to express ourselves. Maybe we are sub-consciously trying to reconnect to our ancestors or tribal beginnings.

ANGELS

Guardian angel(s) are assigned to us at the time of our birth. Some of us only have one, and some of us have two or more. (I have several, and believe me I need them.) They are here to perform God's (Creator's, Spirit's) will, and stay with us throughout our lives. They are not affiliated with a religion or a belief system, in other words, you do not have to be Christian, Jewish, Muslim, etc. to believe in angels or work with them. They help us as we walk our path that we have chosen in this lifetime. Some of us do not realize or acknowledge the fact that our angels are around us all the time. Nevertheless, when we do open ourselves up daily to hear our angels' message(s) and work with them, our lives become more meaningful, peaceful, and spiritual. We have to invite them in everyday, as they are not allowed to intervene or work with us unless we do so. They are only allowed to step in and protect us from imminent danger, but only then.

Archangels:

❖ **Archangel Metatron** is the highest angel in hierarchal standings. His name means "Voice of God." Metatron's cube may be drawn around objects, or draw it around a picture of a person, or visually draw it around a person to ward off evil or negative energies.

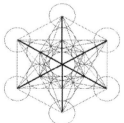

Metatron's cube

❖ **Archangel Michael** is in command of the Army of God, leading forces of good against the darkness of evil. He is in charge of the other archangels. Call upon him to sever the ties, cords, or webbings that attach you to others, as these attachments may be, and probably are, unhealthy for you. His color is Red, his direction is South, his season is Summer, his element is Fire, and he is linked to the 1st Chakra (root chakra).

❖ **Archangel Gabriel** is one of the female archangels. She is the "Messenger of God," sometimes referred to as the "Holy Spirit." Gabriel is protector of women and aids women during childbirth. Her color is Blue, her direction is West, her season is Fall/Autumn, her element is Water, and she is linked to the 5th Chakra (throat chakra).

❖ **Archangel Raphael** is the archangel of healing. Call upon him for healing your emotional, physical, and spiritual self. His color is Green, his direction is North, his season is Winter, and his element is Earth, and he is linked to the 4th Chakra (heart chakra).

❖ **Archangel Uriel** is the "Flame of God" or "Light of God." He is in charge of the heavens and earth. His color is Yellow, his direction is East, his season is Spring, and his element is Air, and he is linked to the 3rd Chakra (solar plexus).

❖ **Archangel Chamuel** is the other female archangel. She represents pure divine love. She will help in your love of self, love of humankind, and your romantic love. Love is a very powerful emotion; it heals, saves, and conquers/overcomes all obstacles. Her color is Pink, and she is linked to the 4th Chakra (heart chakra) also.

❖ **Archangel Jophiel** is the one who guards the Tree of Life in the Garden of Eden. He is said to be the one that is invoked when creating amulets for his protective power. He is also one of the archangels that assist Archangel Michael in fighting battles. His color is Indigo, and he is linked to the 6th Chakra (third eye chakra).

❖ **Archangel Zadkiel** is the archangel of freedom, compassion, and forgiveness. Call upon him to help you in forgiving yourself and forgiving others, so that you have the freedom to move forward on your path to spirituality and enlightenment. He also assists Archangel Michael in fighting battles. His color is Purple or Violet, and he is linked to the 7th Chakra (crown chakra).

❖ **Archangel Azrael** is the "Angel of Death." He is responsible for collecting the human soul at the time of passing on from this earthly domain. He also helps in the death of a matter or issue to help you move on to the next phase of your life or path. His color is Black.

Tip: Call upon the four main archangels (Michael, Gabriel, Raphael, and Uriel) to guard the four corners or directions around you or your home/dwelling/living or work space. They will be there to watch over you and your loved ones by adding their positive loving energy to dispel the negative forces or energies of this realm from harming you and yours.

ANIMAL TOTEMS

Animals may appear to you in your dreams, come into your life physically, or may come to you by way of pictures in a book, magazine, TV, figurines, cloud formations, etc. Animals are nature and we are part of nature. It is natural to have animals become part of or be a part of your existence. These Spirit Guides are your personal connection to Mother Earth and/or the Universe. Animals are here to teach you, to help you grow, to be one with nature, and to walk with you along your path of spiritual awakening; your life's journey. The following animal descriptions are just a few, but this will give you an idea of why a particular animal has appeared in your life. Some of these animals stay with you throughout your lifetime; others come and go when needed.

Aquatic Animals Totems:

❖ **Barracuda** shows how to make your own way and follow your own path with strength and courage.

❖ **Beaver** teaches persistence, durability, emotional balance, builds dreams.

❖ **Catfish** teaches when it is time to discard what is not needed anymore, and to have a greater sensitivity in communication.

❖ **Dolphin** opens new creative dimensions, curiosity, trust, playfulness, and freedom.

❖ **Fish** teaches how to swim the currents of life, use intuition to navigate effectively, and to go with the flow.

❖ **Hippopotamus** teaches how to move gracefully through emotions by balancing the spiritual world with the physical world.

❖ **Sea Horse** teaches caution, patience, and taking on different roles than necessary.

❖ **Starfish** teaches how to maneuver successfully in any situation.

❖ **Whale** teaches how to dive deep within to awaken creativity, imagination, and intuition; also teaches creation, movement, and a strong sense of family.

Birds—Land and Water Totems:

❖ **Blackbird** awakens the mind with awareness, as changes of perceptions are unfolding.

❖ **Bluebird** is about your happiness within and without; she indicates satisfaction, completion, or fulfillment that is happening or about to happen.

❖ **Blue Jay** is highly adaptive and will teach knowledge of survival in this world and in other worlds.

❖ **Buzzard/Vulture** teaches the power of purification of the mind, body, and spirit.

❖ **Cardinal** renews vitality in life and returns joy, brilliance, and balance to mind, body, and spirit.

❖ **Chickadee** is the bird of truth, mind mysteries, and joy. It heals/balances/opens perceptions, and teaches us to use our voice.

❖ **Chicken** is about fertility energies, enthusiasm, new growths, and balancing patience with effort and rewards.

❖ **Crane** is for justice, longevity, female energy, and gives proper focus in all endeavors.

❖ **Crow** is the omen of change—spiritual, mental, and emotional.

❖ **Dove** is the messenger of peace, love, joy, and gentleness, and shows us how to walk between the spiritual and physical world.

❖ **Duck** is for emotional comfort and protection, and aids in balancing the mind and emotions

- ❖ **Eagle** is about creation, mental, spiritual, emotional, swiftness, healing, strength, and wisdom; and aids in seeing hidden spiritual truths.

- ❖ **Flamingo** teaches how to maintain balance and movement through the emotions, and helps in bringing color and vivacity into your life.

- ❖ **Hawk** teaches visionary power and clear sight with strong observation habits.

- ❖ **Hummingbird** teaches joy and fertility.

- ❖ **Kingfisher** is about love and prosperity.

- ❖ **Mockingbird** teaches the art of adaptability and going with the flow.

- ❖ **Owl** is the mystery of silent wisdom, and heightened vision or hearing.

- ❖ **Parrot** teaches listening to all of nature and awakening to the language within by using intuition for open communication.

- ❖ **Peacock** teaches the power of watchfulness, and the strength of mental/emotion/spiritual foundations.

- ❖ **Pelican** demonstrates the power of reflection and insight, and how to ride the air currents of life.

- ❖ **Penguin** teaches grace in emotions and actions.

- ❖ **Pigeon** teaches the importance of home/family.

- ❖ **Quail** teaches about mysticism, and enlightens you about your soul's purpose.

- ❖ **Raven** teaches about the magical act of creation, internal magic, and transformation.

- ❖ **Road Runner** teaches the ability of mental sharpness, quick thinking, and fast responses.

- ❖ **Robin** is about stimulation of new growth and renewal in the many areas of your life.

- ❖ **Rooster** is the guardian, watcher, and protector of family.

- ❖ **Seagull** is the spiritual messenger that demonstrates a higher communication with your guide is taking place.

- ❖ **Sparrow** aids in opening your eyes to your self-worth and instills dignity and empowerment.

- ❖ **Swan** aids in awakening your spirituality and developing your intuition; and also symbolizes love, beauty, and inspiration.

- ❖ **Swift** is all about speed and agility.

- ❖ **Turkey** makes us to be thankful for all blessings, and the vitality and sacredness of life.

- ❖ **Woodpecker** teaches how to connect with Mother Earth and how to ground ourselves in nature.

- ❖ **Wren** teaches to be resourceful and bold.

Insects and Other Critters Totems:

- ❖ **Ant** teaches a sense of community, social structures, and how to plan.

- ❖ **Beetle** aids in transformation, and resurrection/re-birth of one's soul to new spiritual ideals.

- ❖ **Bee** shows one how to communicate and carry heavy loads. Bee also teaches how to develop or create ideas, and to make them productive; bring them to fruition.

Bees are often regarded as symbols of messages from the heavens.

❖ **Butterfly** is a symbol of joy, gentleness, and changes in life. Butterfly is the deliverer of messages between the physical and spiritual worlds.

❖ **Cicada** aids in the endeavor to find the real you; and helps you understand who you are by uncovering hidden truths and secrets that are long forgotten.

❖ **Cockroach** teaches the art of adaptability and ultimate survival instincts.

❖ **Cricket** aids in heightening intuition, sensitivity, and awareness.

❖ **Dragonfly/Damselfly** teaches mastery of moving quickly with precision, breaks down illusions, and heightens visual depth.

❖ **Earthworm** teaches growth, regeneration, healing, and reflection.

❖ **Firefly** teaches how to bring things into focus and to lighten the path that is hidden in order to understand your life-force energy.

❖ **Ladybug** teaches about growth and manifestation of ideas and thoughts.

❖ **Spider** helps in creativity, inspiration, and psychic abilities.

Land Animals Totems:

❖ **Antelope** teaches survival, adaptability of the mind, and is the messenger of a higher purpose.

❖ **Armadillo** teaches about protection and how to use it; also about sensitivity to the attacks of others (real or imagined).

❖ **Bat** teaches that the changes that are taking place are blessings; and to face facts in your life and to trust your instincts.

❖ **Bear** teaches natural healing abilities, leadership, and to defend when necessary.

❖ **Boar/Pig** teaches spiritual strength, protection, and self-reliance.

❖ **Bobcat** teaches there is a time for solitude, and learning to be alone, but not lonely.

❖ **Buffalo** teaches to follow the easiest path, and not to use force, but learn to flow with it.

❖ **Bull** teaches stability without stubbornness.

❖ **Cat** teaches magical or aids you in your magical workings. Cat also teaches you about independence, cleverness, balance of energies, and actions in life.

❖ **Cougar/Mountain Lion** aids one to take charge, be strong, and to come into your own power.

❖ **Cow** teaches about home, community, contentment, and being easy going.

❖ **Coyote** teaches us about wisdom about having fun. Coyote also teaches adaptation and learning from your mistakes.

❖ **Deer** teaches the power of gentleness, love, alertness, and the ability to listen.

* **Dog** teaches protection, companionship, unconditional love, and friendship.

* **Donkey** teaches about patience and humility.

* **Elephant** teaches you about wisdom and power. An elephant helps you with your memory, reclaiming family ideals, and caring for the young and elderly.

* **Fox** teaches cunning, swiftness, persistence, and how to walk in both worlds.

* **Gopher** teaches you how to attune yourself to spiritual and physical vibrations and sensations.

* **Hedgehog** teaches defense mechanisms against negativity, shows how to enjoy life, and walk the earth with lightness and wonder.

* **Horse** teaches travel, freedom, and increase clairvoyance.

* **Mole** teaches sensitivity to your surroundings, and to listen and feel carefully while using your intuition.

* **Polar Bear** deals with death, birth, and transformation of a mystical quality.

* **Porcupine** is good-natured, a reminder of innocence, and trusting in Spirit.

* **Possum** aids in the art to act or behave in a deliberate manner by appearing to be fearful or fearless in spite of your true feelings; gives you the courage to pretend for a while in order to cope mentally and spiritually.

* **Prairie Dog** is the caretaker of everyone in a cooperative environment.

* **Rabbit** helps the artist, enhances sensitivity, and helps in planning for new possibilities.

- ❖ **Raccoon** is about disguise, exploring, and curiosity.

- ❖ **Rat** teaches how to be resourceful in the midst of environmental and emotional change.

- ❖ **Ram** teaches endurance, strength, fortitude, and perseverance in going the distance.

- ❖ **Skunk** teaches you to be respectful, playful, sensual, and to take your time.

- ❖ **Squirrel** teaches gathering and preparedness, awareness, playfulness, and being active in your life.

- ❖ **Wolf** shows loyalty, spirit, strength, friendliness, and intelligence. Wolf also teaches about belong and living in a family/pack.

Reptiles Totems:

- ❖ **Chameleon** teaches how to show true color of self in one's environment and one's sincere emotional nature.

- ❖ **Frog/Toad** is transformation, and teaches how to cleanse and adapt.

- ❖ **Gecko** teaches how to be out-going with tact; and how to overcome obstacles.

- ❖ **Lizard** teaches listening to intuition in dreams, visions, and perceptions.

- ❖ **Tortoise** teaches grounding, patience; and represents wisdom.

- ❖ **Turtle** teaches endurance, survival skills, and patience.

BIRTHSTONES BY ASTROLOGICAL SIGN

Aries: Mar 21 - Apr 20; ruby, amethyst, garnet, topaz, coral

Taurus: Apr 21 - May 20; aquamarine, lapis lazuli, rhodonite

Gemini: May 21 - Jun 20; agate, pearl, chrysoprase, topaz

Cancer: Jun 21 - Jul 22; moonstone, white coral, pearl, emerald

Leo: Jul 23 - Aug 22; amber, diamond, garnet, peridot, topaz

Virgo: Aug 23 - Sept 22; sapphire, agate, jade, amber, citrine

Libra: Sept 23 - Oct 22; aquamarine, moonstone, peridot

Scorpio: Oct 23 - Nov 22; garnet, aquamarine, moonstone, malachite

Sagittarius: Nov 23 - Dec 21; amethyst, lapis lazuli, labradorite, topaz

Capricorn: Dec 22 - Jan 20; amber, amethyst, garnet, onyx, peridot

Aquarius: Jan 21 - Feb 20; opal, garnet, aquamarine

Pisces: Feb 21 - Mar 20; opal aquamarine, moonstone, pearl

BIRTHSTONES BY MONTH[4]

January—Garnet
February—Amethyst
March—Aquamarine
April—Diamond
May—Emerald
June—Pearl

July—Ruby
August—Peridot
September—Sapphire
October—Opal
November—Topaz
December—Turquoise

---

4 The tradition of birthstones may be rooted in the Old Testament of the Bible. The Breastplate of Aaron, a ceremonial garment, was set with 12 stones to represent the 12 tribes of Israel. Thus, you have 12 stones for 12 months.

CANDLEMAS
Also Imbolc, Groundhog Day, St. Brigid's Day

Candlemas, February 2, commemorates the ritual purification of Mary, 40 days after the birth of Christ on December 25. Candlemas is one of the four "cross-quarters" of the year, occurring halfway between the first day of Winter (Winter Solstice) and the first day of Spring (Spring Equinox). Traditionally, it was believe that if Candlemas is sunny, the remaining six weeks of Winter would be stormy and cold. But, if it rained or snowed on Candlemas, the rest of the Winter would be mild. In the US, this is known as Groundhog Day. This day is also called "Imbolc" (pronounced *"im-olk"*), the end of Winter, and the beginning of Spring—a day of newborn calves and lambs, and dormant seeds begin to wake-up within the Earth (Spring has sprung!). With the arrival of these newborns, milk and cheese are once again available for consumption. The promise of the return of light and renewal of life that was made at the Winter Solstice is now starting to show, to come forth and germinate. It is the start of the new planting year, a time for new beginnings.

In the past, it was a custom to bring candles to church to be blessed by the priest on February 2. The candles were then taken home where they served as talismans and protection from all sorts of disasters. This custom was the origin for the name Candlesmass. Originally, this festival was associated with fires that were built in open places. These fires would be lit from the sacred flames (of the previous years' celebration), in which they would be allowed to burn throughout the year. Then, eventually, the fires were built in church courtyards where people would dance around the flames or jump over them. The people would carry home some of the embers to kindle their own fires from the sacred flames. If the observance of Lent starts as early as February 4, this causes Candlemas customs to become associated with Shrove Tuesday, which is also Mardi Gras—Fat Tuesday, or Carnival. The fasting season of Lent, a time of purification, begins on Ash Wednesday, the day after Fat Tuesday.

__Celebration:__ The main element of your decorating scheme for this day is, obviously, candles. Beginning at sundown on Candlemas Eve (Feb 1), gather all the candles in your home into one room and light all of them from one central candle, or place a candle in each window of your home and allow them to continue burning until sunrise (but watch them carefully, don't want any accidents). Or, if you have a fireplace, clean out your hearth, then light a new fire. Have your family and friends sit around the fire or candles to share their hopes for the New Year, like what you hope to accomplish, what your passions are, what you wish to plant in your new garden, etc. Write these ideas down in a journal and/or piece of paper, to make them concrete so that on August 2, the Festival of the First Harvest, Lammas, you can look back to see if, or what progress you have made. Crepes and pancakes are traditional foods for Candlemas because of their round shape and golden color, which are symbols of the sun—the return of light.

__Purification and Renewal:__ You may give up something frivolous or something serious for 40 days (Dec. 25 to Feb. 2), but it should be something that you will miss or notice. Folklore/wisdom says it takes six weeks to establish a new or better habit, so you may end up with a changed or whole new lifestyle.

Spring-cleaning is another act of purification, and since Candlemas is sometimes considered the beginning of Spring, this is a great time to start. This is a good time to get rid of your old things, change your air-conditioner filters, open your windows to let in fresh air, and do a good house cleaning to banish the gloom of Winter and to create a shiny new setting for Spring. A smudge ceremony in your dwelling or workspace this time of year is also a good idea.

CHAKRAS
A Sanskrit term meaning circle or wheel.

✳ **1st Chakra or Root Chakra:** Red—base of the spine; function: grounding, survival, instinct. Singing or humming the musical scale for the 1st Charka is: Do[5] (represents the note C).

✳ **2nd Chakra or Sacral Chakra:** Orange—below the naval; function: creativity, sexual identity, and balance. Singing or humming the musical scale for the 2nd Charka is: Re (represents the note D).

✳ **3rd Chakra or Solar Plexus Chakra:** Yellow—above the naval; function: relationships, connections, trust, emotions. Singing or humming the musical scale for the 3rd Charka is: Mi (represents the note E).

✳ **4th Chakra or Heart Chakra:** Green or Pink—between the breast; function: love, self-acceptance. Singing or humming the musical scale for the 4th Charka is: Fa (represents the note F).

✳ **5th Chakra or Throat Chakra:** Blue—throat area; function: expression, communication. Singing or humming the musical scale for the 5th Charka is: Sol (represents the note G).

---

5 By humming or singing, this musical scale—Do-Re-Mi-Fa-Sol-La-Ti-Do—is an easy way to charge, open up, or align your chakras.

* **6th Chakra or Third Eye Chakra:** Dark Blue or Indigo—brow area, between the eyes; function: clairvoyance/clairaudience, left brain, right brain. Singing or humming the musical scale for the 6th Charka is: La (represents the note A).

* **7th Chakra or Crown Chakra:** Violet, Purple or Clear/White—top of head; function: unity, divinity. Singing or humming the musical scale for the 7th Charka is: Ti (represents the note B).

The chakras are described as energy centers in the body that are located at major branches of the nervous system along the spinal column (they are aligned in an ascending column from the base of the spine to the top of the head). Each chakra is associated with a certain color. They are described as balls of energy moving in a spiraling/circular motion. Or they are sometimes described as lotus flowers with a different number of petals in each chakra. The function of the chakras is to spin and draw in the life-force energy (Chi/Qi/Prana) to keep the spiritual, mental, emotional, and physical health of the body in balance. There is a link between the chakra position and the glands of the endocrine system. The endocrine system is a system of small organs that involve the release of hormones, which are instrumental in regulating your metabolism, growth and development, and tissue function. The endocrine system also plays a part in your moods (i.e., PMS).

 Chakra positions in the body.

Clairvoyance/Clairvoyant

Clairvoyance is the "catch-all" phrase used for the ability to obtain information regarding an object, location, or physical event via means other than the normal human senses. Below, these paranormal senses are broken down into six descriptions for better clarity. *See* Extrasensory Perception (ESP) in this book.

Clairsentience (feeling/touching): Acquiring psychic knowledge primarily via feelings, sensations, or perceptions from people or animals (sentient beings). There are many different levels of clairsentience from having the ability to perceive diseases in people/animals to the thoughts and emotions of people/animals. Psychometry is related to this form of clairvoyance in that information is obtain about an individual by making physical contact with an object that belongs to that particular individual.

Clairaudience (hearing/listening): Clairaudience is having the ability to hear in a paranormal manner, as opposed to paranormal seeing (clairvoyance) and feeling (clairsentience). Clairaudience is an indication of impressions from the "inner mental ear," which is similar to the way people think words, without actually having said these words out loud. It also refers to the actual perception of sounds such as voices, tones, or noises which are not heard by other humans or being able to pick up these sounds via recording equipment. *Example:* A clairaudient person may claim to hear the voices or thoughts of the deceased.

Clairalience (smelling): Clairalience is having the ability to acquire psychic information via means of smelling.

Claircognizance (knowing): Claircognizance is having the ability to acquire psychic information via means of innate knowledge. This is having the ability to know something without knowing why or how one knows it.

Clairgustance (tasting): Clairgustance is having the ability to taste or perceive the essence of a substance without actually placing it in the mouth. A clairgustance person acquires this taste of a substance via the spiritual or otherworldly realms.

__Clairvoyance (seeing):__ Clairvoyance is having the ability to see in a paranormal manner. Someone with this ability is often referred to as a "seer" or having "the sight" or "second sight." They are able to see images in their "mind's eye" or they actually see images of people, animals, etc. They may also see events or happenings from the past or future.

Current thinking among advocates of clairvoyance is that most people are born with clairvoyant abilities, but then they start to subdue or suppress their gift(s) due to outside influence, be it family or peer pressure, because acknowledging this behavior is not the norm nor socially acceptable.

CLEANSING YOUR CRYSTALS/STONES

There are several ways to cleanse your crystals/stones. You may place them in the moonlight, or place the stones in a bowl of sea salt (do not add water, some stones do not do well in water). You may smudge your stone(s). Or, if you know your stone will not dissolve in water, you can hold your stone in running water (be it stream, river, or water faucet), place them in a bowl of water, or you may leave them outside in a rain shower. You may also bury them in soil, either in a pot of soil, or out in your yard/flower bed (just remember where you buried them). You may leave the stone overnight in salt, soil, water, or only do it for 15 to 30 minutes. Let Spirit guide you on this.

COLORS AND THEIR MEANINGS

▲ **Red:** Maintaining health, strength, physical energy, sex, passion, courage, protection, intense emotions, and blood: life/death. Red is associated with the element of Fire and the direction is South. It is the color for Archangel Michael and the Root Chakra, the 1st Chakra.

▲ **Pink:** Love, friendship, compassion, relaxation, and gentle emotions. Pink also overcomes evil, represents honor, love, morality, friendship, and general success. It is the color for Archangel Chamuel and the Heart Chakra, the 4th Chakra.

▲ **Orange:** General attraction, energy, encouragement, strengthens the ability to concentrate, adaptability, and stimulation. Orange is the color of the Sacral Chakra, the 2nd Chakra. By calling in Archangels Michael and Uriel (red + yellow = orange), they would be the ones to help with healing/energizing this chakra.

▲ **Yellow:** Intellect, confidence, divination, communication, eloquence, travel, movement, attraction, persuasion (can change minds), instills confidence, and charm. Yellow is associated with the element of Air and the direction is East. It is the color for Archangel Uriel and the Solar Plexus Chakra, the 3rd Chakra.

▲ **Green:** Money, prosperity, employment, fertility, healing, growth, luck, financial success, and cooperation. Green is associated with the element of Earth and the direction is North. It is the color for Archangel Raphael and the Heart Chakra, the 4th Chakra.

▲ **Blue:** Healing, peace, intuitiveness, patience, happiness. Blue is associated with the element Water and the direction is West. It is the color for Archangel Gabriel and the Throat Chakra, the 5th Chakra.

▲ **Dark Blue:** Changeability, impulsiveness, and intuition. Dark blue is also referred to as indigo and is the color of the 3rd-Eye Chakra, the 6th Chakra. It is the color for Archangel Jophiel.

▲ **Light Blue:** Understanding, health, tranquility, peace, protection, general happiness, sharpens the power to perceive, spiritual awareness, and patience.

▲ **Purple:** Power, healing severe disease, spirituality, meditation, religion, ambition, promotes business progress, power: worldly, psychic or magical, and strengthens will power. Purple is associated with the

Crown Chakra, the 7th Chakra. It is the color for Archangel Zadkiel.

▲ **White:** Protection, purification, used for all purposes. It is symbolic of the Moon. Adds to spiritual strength, breaks curses, or crossed conditions. It represents faith, purity, truth, and sincerity. Because white contains all colors, it may be utilized for every magical purpose. White is also a color associated with the Crown Chakra, the 7th Chakra.

▲ **Black:** Banishing negativity, absorbing negativity, and wisdom. It is symbolic of the universe/outer space. It is used to represent death, but this is death of a matter or issue, so that you may move on to the next phase of your path. This is not an evil color. It is the color for Archangel Azrael.

▲ **Brown:** Animals. Used for spells involving animals, usually in combination with other colors. Brown represents soil and fertility of the Earth. Brown means hesitation in all matters, uncertainty and doubt, or neutrality.

▲ **Gray:** Cancellation, stalemate, or neutrality.

CUCHULAINN
(Pronounced "Ku-HOO-lin")

In Celtic lore, Culann, the smith, invites Conchobar, the king, to a feast at his house. Before going, Conchobar goes to the playing field to watch the young boys play hurling. He is so impressed by Sétanta, one of the young boys, that he asks Sétanta to join him at the feast. Sétanta replied that he would join him as soon as the game is over. Conchobar forgets to inform Culann that Sétanta will be joining them, and Culann lets loose his ferocious guard dog to protect his house. When Sétanta arrives, the enormous dog attacks him, but he kills the dog in self-defense. Culann is devastated by the loss of his dog. Sétanta promises he will replace the dog, but until then he himself will guard Culann's house. From that time forward, Sétanta was called Cú Chulainn (Culann's Hound). Cuchulain became the Irish hero who single-handedly defended Ulster against the armies of Queen Maeve. He was son of the God Lugh and Deichtine, who was the sister of the King of Ulster.

DIVINATION

Divination is the method of acquiring knowledge of the unknown or the future by interpreting omens or signs. There are many methods of divination, to mention a few, they are: Crystal gazing; dreams or visions; automatic writing; astrology; tea leaves; communicating with the spirits; tarot; runes; scrying; palmistry; I Ching; telepathy; dowsing; pendulum; talking board (Ouija); séance; ESP, clairvoyance; or gazing into fire or the flame of a candle.

EAR CANDLING

Ear Candling, also referred to as "Ear Coning," is an ancient healing method believed to have originated in Egypt and is still in use today through alternative medicine and holistic centers. Ear candling[6] is a natural way to clear earwax from the ears and sinuses by drawing out impurities from the ear canal via a hollow ear candle. The pointed or tapered end of the candle is placed in (not forced) into the ear opening. The opposite end is lit, and while it is burning, you will hear crackling noises in your ear as the impurities are pulled out. As the flame seeks oxygen, it forms a vacuum in the hollow ear candle, causing the wax, toxins, and impurities to be pulled out of the ear up into the candle. It is not a difficult process, but you should have someone help you with this by keeping watch over the burning candle. Your metaphysical or holistic healing shops will be able to assist you in your needs or questions regarding ear candling.

---

6   For more information and step-by-step instructions go to http://healing.about.com/od/earcandling/Ear_Candling.htm.

ELEMENTS: AIR/FIRE/WATER/EARTH

There a four elements used in magic that correspond to the four directions: East—*Air*, South—*Fire*, West—*Water*, and North—*Earth*. They are also used for the four quarters of the magical circle (Spring, Summer, Fall, and Winter). Fire and Air are male energies with Water and Earth being female energies. Each element is associated with a color: *East*—Yellow; *South*—Red; *West*—Blue; *North*—Green. Each element resonates/connects with different parts or functions of your body—*Earth* is bone; *Air* is breath; *Water* is blood; and *Fire* is sprit.

❖*Air:* Air represents mental activity, thoughts, reason and intellect, memory, knowledge, persuasion, birth and friendship, freedom, clarification, and expression. A low air person seems without any direction and unable to define or visualize any future, and cannot understand the choices or outcomes. A high air person is at ease in complex situations and can sit and think things through, and carry through with decisions.

Air Info: Its feelings are moist heat, Spring is the season, and its direction is East/mental. Its symbols are the wand or athame[7] (knife), or the smoke of incense; its colors are white, light blues, yellows, and greens. The moon phase is the first quarter, and its time is dawn. Air magic is visualization (thoughts), making the events happen by fixing the images or ideas in one's mind. Words are put together to form spells, prayers, affirmations, or used in channeling one's power giving rise to desires that can be released upon the winds for attainment (but there is no need to say aloud). Mirror magic, a scrying tool, helps with personal decisions by using both word and visualization to aid in being able to visualize future event(s). Air is Chi or Qi in character—life-force energy or spiritual energy. The archangel of Air is Uriel and the elementals are sylphs. Air's place on the pentacle is the upper, right point. *Alchemical or Magical Symbol for Air:* △

---

7 Athame is pronounced "æ-tha-may" or "æ-thām"

❖ *Fire:* Fire represents passion, enthusiasm, desire and courage, force, lust, fertility and virility, initiative, and rejuvenation. A low fire person is usually cold, slow to act, and without enthusiasm for life, or oneself. A high fire person is bold, dramatic, and passionate in all areas within oneself; however, this person must be careful, as fire can destroy everything in its path.

Fire Info: Its feelings are hot and dry, Summer is the season, direction is South/energy. Its symbol is the athame or sword, candle, charcoal, fire, or burner/cauldron; its colors are reds, oranges, and golds. The moon phase is the second quarter, and its time is high-noon. Fire magic (Sun magic) is used to bring about new ideas, new beginnings, attracting your desires, and is used to destroy the old. It also represents courage and passion. Fire is Yang/masculine in character. The archangel of Fire is Michael and the elementals are salamanders, phoenix, or dragons. Fire's place on the pentacle is the lower, right point.

Alchemical or Magical Symbol for Fire: △

❖ *Water:* The symbol of our emotions, it occupies all life forms. Water engages intuition, insight, fertility, the womb, health, beauty, and divination. A low water person appears indifferent and unresponsive to life. But, with a high water person, it seems that with the slightest touch or look their faucet will open, and they become overly emotional or dramatic. The person with a good balance of water keeps the flow running efficiently.

Water Info: Its feelings are cold moisture, Fall is the season, direction is West/emotion. Its symbols are the cup or chalice and its colors are blues, sea greens, light grays, and whites. The moon phase is the full moon, and its time is dusk. Water magic involves the use of rivers, lakes, or beaches, and the use of sand, shells, rocks, animals, and freshwater/seawater. Water from your faucet is also good to use, just let it stand for 24-hours before using, if possible. Or, put some water in a bowl, set it outside in the full moon to be charged with Her magic to use for future workings. Or, just letting the water flow from your faucet for a few seconds before putting into a bowl is also good. Remember, the intent is always there. Water magic may also involve the use of a scrying bowl. This is a dark bowl filled with clear water, which you are able to gaze into to visualize the future or future events or to help clarify decisions. Water is Yin/feminine in character. The archangel of Water is Gabriel and the elementals are undines/mermaids. Water's place on the pentacle is the lower, left point.

Alchemical or Magical Symbol for Water: ▽

❖ ***Earth:*** Earth is the source and provider of all our needs. It represents sensations, decay, patience, stability, strength, health, warmth, comfort, animals and animal instincts, gardening, and physical labor. A low earth person may seem confused, insecure and alone, unable to feel wanted, and their work can become affected with such feelings. A high earth person is practical, quite, down to earth, hard worker, stable, and a good provider, but can also be a little too stubborn at times.

Earth Info: Its feeling is dry and cold, its season is Winter, direction is North/body. Its symbols are the pentacle, salt, grain, soil, or a stone such as jasper, and its colors are browns, blacks, purples, and greens. The moon phase is the new moon, and its time is midnight. Earth magic involves the use of herbs/plants. Using the correct herb(s) along with the other tools mentioned to attain one's desire, can be very effective. Earth is a balance of both Yin and Yang. The archangel of Earth is Raphael and the elementals are gnomes/goblins/satyrs. Earth's place on the pentacle is the top point. (Spirit's place on the pentacle is the upper, left point.)

Alchemical or Magical Symbol for Earth: ▽

EMPATHY/EMPATH

Empathy is having the capability to comprehend and understand people and be in sync with or to resonate with others, voluntarily or involuntarily. An empath is able to scan a person's psyche for thoughts and feelings, and can also "see or feel" that person's past, present, or future life occurrences. Empaths also experience empathy towards pets, plants, and inanimate objects.

EXTRASENSORY PERCEPTION (ESP)

ESP is having the ability to receive information via paranormal or mystical means. Information may be acquired by telepathy, is sensing of thoughts or feelings; precognition is knowledge of future events; and clairvoyance is awareness of people, objects, or events. ESP may also be referred to as "one's sixth sense" such as having a gut instinct, a hunch, a weird vibe, or an intuition. *See* Clairvoyance/Clairvoyant in this book.

FENG SHUI

An ancient Chinese practice that utilizes the laws of both Heaven/Astronomy and Earth/Geography to help the improvement of one's life by encouraging positive Qi/Chi, the flow of energy. Feng shui, pronounced *"fung shway,"* literally translates as "wind-water" in English.

Modern feng shui schools teach the practice of arranging objects, as in the placement of furniture in one's home or office. It is also the use of plants, flowers, and stones in the home, office, and landscape to achieve harmony with the environment. It may be used for choosing a place to live, picking a burial site, or for agricultural planning. Feng shui has a positive effect on one's health, wealth, and personal relationships.

A bagua map is a tool used by a feng shui consultant to map a room, home, or office. It shows how the different sections correspond to different aspects in one's life. The map is divided into categories such as fame, relationships, marriage, children, creativity, careers, etc. The map will aid the consultant in finding the areas that may be lacking good Chi. It shows the negative or absent spaces that may need correcting to enhance one's life and the environment.

Example: If the bagua map is placed over the layout of the house and it shows the toilet, bathroom, laundry, or kitchen in the wealth/blessings area, it would be considered that the money coming into that particular environment would disappear very fast (i.e., money going down the drain). By placing mirrors in certain areas (behind the toilet, behind the sink, etc.) of that room, the mirror would discourage this from happening. Closing the toilet lid when flushing, keeps the good Chi energy from being flushed out of the home, room, or office.

BAGUA MAP

Life Situation Wealth, Prosperity Element: Wind Color: Blue/Purple/Red	Life Situation Fame, Reputation, or Rank Element: Fire Color: Red	Life Situation Love, Relationships, or Mother Element: Earth Color: Red/Pink/White
Life Situation Family, Health, Friends, or Past Element: Wood Color: Blue/Green	**Health & Well- being Yin/Yang**	Life Situation Children, Creativity, or Future Element: Metal Color: White
Life Situation Knowledge, Wisdom or Spirituality Element: Hills or Mountains Color: Black/Blue/Green	Life Situation Career Element: Water Color: Black	Life Situation Helpful people, Travel, or Father Element: Heaven Color: White/Gray/Black

↑

Align this column with the entrance of the home, room, or particular area

FRIDAY THE 13TH AND NUMBER 13

It is estimated, that in the United States some $800 to $900 million are lost in business each Friday the 13th, due to some people not willing to travel or work this day. It is not known how the superstition for Friday the 13th started. Numerologists consider 12 a complete number: 12 months in a year, 12 signs of the zodiac, 12 Gods of Olympus, 12 tribes of Israel, and 12 apostles of Jesus. This may be the cause for the superstition surrounding number 13, but we are not for sure. Some believe it started with the painting "The Last Supper" depicting Jesus and the disciples. Judas, the one standing by Jesus, is the 13th disciple and the one who betrays Jesus. This may have started the superstition or mystique with the number 13 and with Friday the 13th, as Jesus was soon killed afterwards.

Also, with Friday named after Frigg (sometimes called Freya), the Norse Goddess of Love and Sex, it caused a distrust of Fridays in the early Church's overall opposition to Pagan religions. With this strong female figure posing a threat to the male-dominated Christian religion, and to fight the Goddess' influence, the Church characterized her as a witch, thus prompting the fear for the day named after her. Also, in some pagan cultures, Friday was the Sabbat, a day of worship. Once Christianity entered the scene, Freya whose sacred animal was a cat, was re-cast in folklore as a witch, thus causing the fear of witches. Even though Friday the 13th superstition is older than the 14th century, there is another theory that it began on Friday, October 13, 1307, when France's King Philip IV arrested members of the Knights Templar. The Knights Templar are said to be the founders of the military orders, accused them of heresy and tortured them into making confessions with some of them being executed.

In the 18th century, according to legend, the British Navy commissioned a ship called the H.M.S. Friday in order to quell the superstition. The navy selected the crew on a Friday, launched the ship on a Friday and even selected a man named James Friday as the ship's captain. Then, one Friday morning, the ship set off on its maiden voyage never to be seen again. Because of this, British sailors during this period were very superstitious of Friday and often refused to ship out to sea on that day.

The Apollo 13 space mission brought the number 13 to the forefront of the American public. It was launched at 1313 hours (USA Central Time), from launch pad 39 (3 x 13), and was aborted on April 13, 1970. In England, both Friday and the number 13, at one time, were closely associated with capital punishment. Friday was the day for public hangings, with 13 steps leading to the noose. And, if you have 13 letters in your name, you may be considered unlucky: Jack the Ripper, Charles Manson, Jeffrey Dahmer, and Theodore Bundy all have 13 letters in their names.

In ancient Goddess religions, 13 was a lucky number because it corresponded to the number of lunar (menstrual) cycles in a year (13 x 28 = 364 days). There are also 13 members of a Wiccan coven in order to cast a circle or gathering of the coven. The 13th person would be the priest/priestess. It is no surprise that the number 13, being a sacred number to most Pagan traditions, was considered evil by early Christians.

On the other hand, the ancient Egyptians considered 13 lucky, because they believed life unfolded in 12 stages, and that there was a 13th stage—the afterlife, the beyond. Number 13 symbolized death as a happy transformation. In a Tarot deck, the "Death" card bears the number 13, but has a positive meaning, which is transformation.

Paraskevidekatriaphobia is a morbid, irrational fear of Friday the 13th. It is a term coined by therapist Dr. Donald Dossey. He claims that when and if you can pronounce the word you are cured. Triskaidekaphobia, which is related to paraskevidekatraphobia, is the fear of the number 13. For those of you having a fear of Friday the 13th, you may want to consider turning off the alarm and just staying in bed all day.

GEMSTONES: MEANINGS AND HEALING PROPERTIES

Crystals and gemstones have been used for thousands of years for their healing properties and to attract certain positive energies. Gemstones and crystals are able to absorb, transmit, amplify, and focus energy. Crystals and gemstones can lighten one's spirit and/or calm and balance one's mind. Loose stones may be carried in your pocket (or somewhere on your person: I place mine in my bra, just remember they are there before you take off your bra) to receive the vibrational energy of the stone. You may also place the stone(s) under your pillow or by your bed at night to absorb the energy of the stone(s). Some energy healers (Reiki practitioners, massage therapists, etc.) use stones in their practice to increase the energy healing session by placing stones on the body of the person that they are working with. The healer may also place the stones near the person they are healing by placing them under the massage table or just on the table itself, so that the vibrational healing of the stones are absorbed during the session.

If a stone does not feel right—by receiving negative vibrations, energies, or thoughts while working with it, you need to put it aside by burying it in the ground, and giving it back to Mother Earth for her to work her healing energy/magic on the stone. After burying it, walk away from it, not to be used by you again. This does not happen often, but some stones pick up negative energy and they are not ready or meant to be used. The following is just a small list of crystals and gemstones and their properties. The ones listed are what I have in my collection and what I use for healing or have in my home because of their energy, beauty, and charm. There are many more wonderful stones not listed that are very useful as well.

Gemstones:

❖ **Agate—All Purpose Stone:** Agates have protective qualities and guards the wearer from all dangers. Agates provide the wearer with a bold heart. It allows self-expression in a peaceful manner and aids in shyness. It assists in creating peace of mind, so that reason and intuition may be blended. Use this stone to learn acceptance of yourself and others.

- ❖ **Amazonite—Self-Expression Stone:** Amazonite calms mental and emotional chaos by helping you to blend facts with intuitive wisdom. It increases creative expression, promotes kindness, and level-headedness. Amazonite will assist the wearer with courage of self-expression.

- ❖ **Amber—Gentle Stone:** Amber was one of the first stones used for decoration, amulets, and medicinal purposes. Amber is a highly calming stone that relieves depression. It is also used as a protective shield against taking on another person's pain.

- ❖ **Amethyst—Master Healer Crystal:** Amethyst is a stone of spirituality and contentment. It works to build spiritual awareness, intuition, self-worth, and spiritual peace, and it allows the possibility of change. Amethyst aids in meditation, stress relief, and helps with alleviating insomnia.

- ❖ **Aquamarine—Fearless Stone:** Aquamarine strengthens, heals, calms, and balances. It helps against fears, phobias, and stress. It is an opener of the heart and throat by allowing emotional understanding and expression of self, allowing you to speak your heart, and express your true self to others.

- ❖ **Carnelian—Self-Esteem Stone:** Carnelian symbolizes creativity, sexuality, emotions, and intuition. It increases physical energy, power, and creativity. It also helps the wearer discover her personal talents, and assists in decision-making. It promotes courage, action and movement, concentration, determination, and self-confidence.

- ❖ **Chrysocolla—Forgiveness Stone:** Chrysocolla is an important gemstone to use for releasing grief, sadness, guilt, and fear. By doing so, it allows you to bring in forgiveness, joy, certainty, peace, and balance.

❖ **Chrysoprase—Acceptance Stone:** Chrysoprase activates and energizes the heart. It helps to lift the emotions, release tension, and stress. Promotes self-acceptance, acceptance of others, and supports inner growth. It also helps with success in new enterprises. It also activates your artistic abilities, if they have become stagnant.

❖ **Citrine—Success Stone:** Citrine, called "the merchant stone," it aids in accumulating wealth and in achieving success in your profession. Men are drawn to citrine for the courage and self-discipline it offers. Getting tasks done, developing self-worth, and mastering the ego may be achieved through the energies of citrine.

❖ **Coral—Encouragement Stone:** Coral quiets the emotions and dispels feelings of gloom and sadness. It encourages a passionate energy.

❖ **Emerald—Prosperity Stone:** Emeralds bring out traits such as loyalty, sensitivity, and passion. It softens arrogance, promotes harmony, and organization. It is good for stimulating the intellect and memory when you need to make important choices. It also represents abundance, balance, intelligence, re-birth, and maturity.

❖ **Hematite—Emotional Support Stone:** Hematite helps with self-esteem and self-confidence. It is used to protect one's self against negativity by reflecting it back to the sender. It protects people who have difficulty in preventing themselves from absorbing the emotions of others. Hematite is very grounding. If you have a hard time focusing, staying with projects, etc., this is a good stone to use.

❖ **Iolite—Self-Exploration Stone:** Iolite encourages curiosity and achievement by enhancing spiritual exploration and awakening inner knowledge.

❖ **Jade—Good Luck Stone:** Jade is a deep-heart healing gemstone. Use it for all issues of the heart and love. It promotes compassion, aids health, and prevents sickness. It provides calming, stability, soothing effects, and encourages serenity and harmony. It is also a great stone to use when you need grounding to get you through the day.

❖ **Jasper—Nurturing Stone:** Jasper brings the energy of the sun down to rejuvenate and strengthen the body. It relieves stress and connects us to our inner strength and flow. It helps promote intuition, sensitivity, and calmness.

❖ **Labradorite—Enlightenment Stone:** Labradorite provides understanding of the destiny one has chosen, higher consciousness, patience, freedom, and meditation.

❖ **Lapis Lazuli—Balancing Stone:** Lapis lazuli is a stabilizer, changing negative views of reality to positive views. It cleanses the mind, stimulates mental strength, and intellectual precision. It is the stone of contemplation and meditation. It is considered a stone of truth and friendship.

❖ **Mahogany Obsidian—Healer of Unworthiness Issues Stone:** Mahogany Obsidian cleanses the 2nd Chakra of negative energies that are from old wounds. It is ideal in helping one dispel feelings of unworthiness and it shields one from psychic attacks, it's like having an etheric bodyguard.

❖ **Malachite—Stone of Transformation:** Malachite provides powerful deep healing! It clears repressed emotions, releases old pains, and protects against negativity. It calms the anxiety that accompanies physical disease so that healing may take place. It gives balance, and enhances creativity and change. It promotes success and wealth by removing obstacles to one's growth.

❖ **Moonstone—Female Stone:** Moonstone is a talisman of good fortune and is regarded as a sacred stone. It increases intuition, soothes the mind, and aids in spiritual development. The moonstone is definitely female in nature and is beneficial to women. For those who feel overwhelmed by their emotions, it helps to create a balance. For those out of touch with their feelings, it brings them into awareness. It is also used for protection against the perils of travel.

❖ **Mother of Pearl—Stone of Sincerity:** Mother of pearl signifies faith, charity, and innocence. It enhances personal integrity and helps provide focus. It has been used to provide a reflection of the self so that you become aware of how you appear to others.

❖ **Obsidian—Balancing Stone:** Obsidian helps balance one's body, mind, and spirit. It works fast and with great power. Obsidian is a strong protective stone that forms a shield around the wearer to repel negative energy. Placing it under your pillow or by your bed while you sleep is said to draw out the day's stress and tension to be replaced with calming positive energy. Be sure to cleanse it each time after using it for this purpose.

❖ **Onyx—Protective Stone:** Onyx, one of the most powerful protection stones, helps in emotional stability and determination. It offers understanding, confidence, and friendship. It absorbs and transforms negative energy. It is used to banish grief, enhance self-control, help with decision-making, and encourage happiness. It is believed to cool the ardors of love, thus it helps people who cannot let go of past relationships to release them.

❖ **Opal—Mystic Stone:** Opals are water stones, and like to be bathed in cold water. This stone enhances one's psychic and mystical visions. It makes you aware of your self-worth and helps in learning your full potential. Opals are used to regulate insulin, aid women in childbirth, and aids with PMS.

❖ **Pearl—Luna Stone:** The Pearl is a symbol of the moon and its magical powers.

❖ **Peridot—Healing Stone:** Peridot is a bright green gemstone that gives you a warm and friendly energy. It cleanses and stimulates the heart. It brings openness and acceptance to matters of the heart, love, and relationships. It heals anger, jealousy, hurt feelings, low self-esteem, and wounded egos. It reduces depression, cures grudges, and helps repair deteriorated relationships. It is a powerful amulet against evil.

❖ **Quartz—Master Healer Stone:** Quartz is the most powerful stone of all the crystals and gemstones. It is found worldwide. It absorbs, amplifies, and releases energy. It is an all-purpose healing stone. Holding a quartz crystal in your hand increases your natural energy, stimulates your immune system, and balances your chakras. There are many uses for quartz crystals.

❖ **Rhodochrosite—Love Stone:** Rhodochrosite is the gemstone of love and balance. It cleanses the heart and body by releasing suffering and anxiety. It brings one joy and heals chronic self-blame. It promotes love towards life and others. It brings emotional balance to love relationships.

❖ **Rhodonite—Acceptance Stone:** Rhodonite helps you to achieve your greatest potential. It dispels anxiety and promotes rationality. It represents the relationship of yourself with your own body in order to listen to it and love it despite its limitations.

❖ **Rutilated Quartz—Transmission Stone:** Rutilated quartz eases depression, facilitates communication, increases clairvoyance, transmutes negativity, and enhances communication with spirit guides. It is a great physical healer.

❖ **Sapphire—Wisdom Stone:** Sapphire balances emotional influences by giving clarity and inspiration. It enhances will power and faith in judgment.

❖ **Serpentine—Meditation Stone:** Serpentine is an exceptional meditation stone. It assists in finding inner peace and clears the mind to become closer to your inner-self. It is said to protect one against snakebites, poisoning, and magical spells.

❖ **Smoky Quartz—Stone of Power & Harmony:** Smoky Quartz is a crystal for protection and awareness. It gives stability and security. It heals fears, addictions, discouragement, and depression. It promotes personal pride and joy in living. It helps to process one's negative beliefs and gives courage and confidence to make changes. It is very grounding.

❖ **Sodalite—Stone of Peace:** Sodalite calms the emotions and clears the mind of emotional confusion so that rational thinking may occur. It dispels irrelevant thoughts, provides mental focus, and maintains logical reasoning. It helps you relax and helps restore your energies (physic and physical). It is very good for people who tend to be re-active and oversensitive.

❖ **Sugilite—Security Stone:** Sugilite helps release anger, guilt, insecurity, and resentment. It puts you in touch with your inner source of strength and light.

❖ **Sunstone—Happiness Stone:** Sunstone helps you to discover your life's purpose. It evokes courage and heals fear. It dispels sadness and fills you with joyful energy.

❖ **Tiger's Eye—Calming Stone:** Tiger's Eye is a great protection stone. It releases negative energy from your body, and produces soothing vibrations that generate calmness to remove turmoil from your life. It enhances patience, and helps you to focus and concentrate.

❖ **Tiger Iron—Energy Stone:** Is a combination of Jasper, Hematite, and Tiger's Eye. It is helpful for those who are exhausted on any level (body, mind, and spirit). It works on the blood by balancing the red-white cell count and eliminates toxins. Keep it in contact with the skin to accomplish this.

❖ **Topaz—Abundance Stone:** Topaz is a powerful healing stone that relieves tension, pain, and disease. It helps break up stagnant energy within the body and assists with the elimination of toxins. Its strong magnetic energy attracts love, prosperity, and enhances creativity. It enables the communication of your feelings in a powerful manner and leads to inspiration and confidence.

❖ **Tourmaline—Comfort Stone:** Tourmaline brings deep comforting love and energy. It heals fear and panic, and brings in a sense of security and safety. It is able to transform your negative behavior into positive behavior, or to rid you of your old belief patterns. It is a good gemstone to help a person recover from abuse. Black tourmaline is good for jet lag.

❖ **Turquoise—Talisman for Good Fortune & Protection:** Turquoise is a very sacred stone used for centuries by Native Americans. It brings peace, serenity, and tranquility. It heals sadness and grief, and aids you in developing inner strength.

GODDESS BRIGHID
Also Brigid/Brigit, St. Brigid, or St. Brigit

Brigid/Brighid is perhaps one of the most revered and complex Goddesses of the Celtic pantheon. Brighid is the Goddess of healing, divination, prophecy, poets/bards, and smiths or smithcraft/blacksmith. All of these are practical gifts that inspire wisdom. The role of the smith in the tribe or clan was seen as sacred and was associated with magical powers, as it involved mastering the element of Fire to smelt the mineral from the Earth into metal for molding through skill, knowledge, and strength. And with the use of Water for cooling the metal and Air to keep the Fire going, Smithcraft is connected to stories concerning the creation of the world by using all of the Elements (Earth, Air, Fire, and Water) to create and fuse a new shape. She had two sisters, who were also named Brighid, with the three of them making up the classic Triple Goddess, all working as one Goddess, but emitting three different roles when necessary.

Brigid is honored during the celebration of Imbolc (pronounced *"im-olk"*), also known as St. Brigit's Day (Feb. 2), which represents the birth of new spring lambs/calves, fresh milk, spring rains, and new beginnings. She is also associated with fertility magic. Imbolc is celebrated by Pagans, Candlemas by Christians, and in America we have Groundhog Day. This day is used to mark the end of Winter, as rivers, springs, and lakes are starting to thaw, lambs and calves are born, flowers are coming up, etc. During this time of year, She is honored by lighting candles and decorating wells. If there are no wells close by, the strips of cloth/ribbon may be placed outside the doors of the dwellings on Imbolc Eve for Brigid to bless. The strips may then be used for healing throughout the year. Along with the strips of cloth, a bowl of fresh milk may be placed by the well or outside the door in her honor.

Wells are fed by underground springs, which feed the lakes and rivers that run into the oceans/seas, and with Earth being made up of approx. 70-percent water, this means that to honor Brigid, is to also honor Mother Earth.

Brigid/Brigit has been revered by the Celts as a Saint for more than fourteen hundred years, and as a Goddess long before the Romans set foot in Britain and even before the birth of Christ. The worship of her was so powerful that the Celtic Christian Church had to set her up as a Saint. The Roman Catholic Church, at a later date, had to follow suit because her followers would not give her up. Along with St. Patrick, St. Brigit is the patron Saint of Ireland.

Anvil: The blacksmith's tool or any of the tools of the trade are appropriate symbols to honor the Goddess/Saint.

Colors: *White* the color of purity and the color of milk and milk products are associated with Brigid. *Red* is the color of the hearth fire. *Blue*, in the Christian sense, is the color of her mantle/cloak, which is representative of the Virgin Mary. *Green*, which is said to also be the color of her cloak, is associated with faeries and Ireland.

Feasts: St. Brigit's Feast is also referred to as Candlemas (Imbolc). Candlemas is a time when St. Brigit blesses candles. A blessed, three-wick, white candle may be dedicated to her and kept on your alter in honor of her.

Raven: This bird is associated with Imbolc or St. Brigit's Feast, as it is the first bird to nest in the Highlands of Scotland around February 1.

Sacred Woods: St. Brigit and Goddess Brigid are both said to have carried a white wand made from birch or willow. Also, in the Catholic tradition, her prayer cards depict her sacred wood as a vine. The church of Kildare, her church/monastery, was built at the site of a traditional Druid oak grove (oak being sacred to the Druids).

Symbols: Brigid's symbol is the Greek Caduceus for healing. The number nineteen is known as her sacred number. At one time, there were nineteen virgins in the monastery at Kildare, Ireland, who kept a perpetual flame going in her honor. The number three is also sacred to Brigid, as it represents the "Triple Goddess."

St. Brigit's Cross: This is an equal arm cross made from straw or corn husk to represent the salvation of Jesus Christ. The cross is hung above the front door of the dwelling for protection, and also hung above the beds of children for the same reason. The old cross should be burned in the fires on St. Brigit's Eve, Imbolc Eve, or Candlemas Eve, with a new one being made on St. Brigit's Feast Day, Imbolc, or Candlemas for her blessings and protection in the New Year.

St. Brigit's Cross

GODDESS ISIS

Isis is an ancient Egyptian Goddess who taught her people how to read, make bread, beer, weave cloth, and was the benefactor of nature and magic. She is also the Goddess of medicine and wisdom. Isis is the first daughter of Geb, the Earth God, and Nut, the Sky Goddess. Isis married her brother Osiris—Egyptian God of the Dead; she is also the mother of Horus. Isis is the Egyptian Goddess of Re-birth, the ideal mother and wife, and representative of everything feminine.

GODDESS QUAN YIN OR KWAN YIN

Quan Yin or Kwan Yin is known as the Goddess of Mercy. She was originally male until the early part of the 12th century and has evolved from that time as a male Indian bodhisattva—the merciful lord of utter enlightenment—to a Chinese Goddess of mercy. She chose to remain on earth to bring relief to the suffering, rather than enjoy the ecstasies of Nirvana. One of the several stories surrounding Quan Yin is that she was a Buddhist who, through great love and sacrifice during her life, earned the right to enter Nirvana after death. However, while standing before the gates of Paradise, she heard a cry of anguish from the Earth below. Turning back to earth, she renounced her reward of eternal bliss, but in its place found immortality in the hearts of the suffering. She is compared to the Virgin Mary, at times.

Worshipped especially by women, Kwan Yin comforts the troubled, the sick, the lost, the senile, and the unfortunate. She cares for souls in the underworld, and is invoked during post-burial rituals to free the souls of the deceased from the torments of purgatory. Worshippers request her to bring children, generally sons, but if the mother asks for a daughter, she will be beautiful.

Quan Yin is usually depicted as a barefoot, gracious woman dressed in a beautiful, white flowing robe, with a white hood gracefully draped over the top of her head and carrying a small upturned vase of holy dew. She stands tall and slender, a figure of infinite grace, and her gently composed features conveying sublime selflessness and compassion have made her the favorite of all deities. Sometimes she is portrayed as riding a mythological animal known as the Hou, which resembles a Buddhist lion, and symbolizes the divine supremacy exercised by Quan Yin over the forces of nature.

HAG STONES
Also called Fairy Stones, Wish Stones, Witch Stones, Holey Stones, or Holy Stones

Hag stones are found in rivers, creeks, streams, beaches, etc. They are powerful because the hole is carved by the power of nature, which cause these stones to be imparted with the wisdom and magic of Mother Earth and the spirit world.

According to Italian Witchcraft, the holed stones are also associated with fairies and are a doorway into the fairy kingdom. In Italian Witchcraft, the stones are considered to bring the finder good luck and fortune and are a seen as a favor from the Goddess Diana. Diana is the Goddess of hunt, wild animals, the woodlands or forests, and she is associated with the moon, a Lunar Goddess.

These powerful stones are said to be able to bestow the holder psychic powers when looking through the hole of the stone. If you look through the hole during the light of the full moon, you are able to see the fairy realm and possibly ghosts or visions of the "other world."

When the hag stone is worn or carried, it wards off evil spirits, evil eye, or those wishing to do you harm. It is a protection against black magic and evil hags (evil witches), to bad Snow White didn't have one.

If the stones are hung from the bedposts or placed under the mattress or bed, they will prevent nightmares from visiting the sleeper. The stones are also used in the protection of animals especially farm animals, by placing the stone around their necks or by hanging the stone in their stalls. The stones are used to protect cows' milk from going sour during thunderstorms, as evil spirits are most active then. The stones are thought to keep the "evil hag" (evil witch) from stealing the horses or causing harm to them.

Hand-carved, large holey stones, called "men-an-tols," were used in ancient ceremonies to represent the doorway between the physical and spiritual world. These large stones were placed at the entrance of tombs and cairns,[8] and thought to represent the re-birth transition. Ancient Celts held marriage ceremonies with the new couple joining hands through the hole in the stone to bless the union. The couple, after a year of marriage, could choose to return to the stone and renounce the union without any remorse or animosity towards each other and the dissolving of the marriage.

Hag stones are cleansed or cleared in the same manner as crystals and gemstones. *See* Cleansing Your Crystals/Stones in this book.

---

8 Cairns are loose piles of stones that are erected as burial chambers or to mark tombs, and as portals to other worlds. Cairns are made at regular intervals along paths or hiking trails as landmarks to show the way and are maintained by groups of hikers adding a stone when they pass. They are also used to represent a place of importance.

HALLOWEEN
Also All Saints' Day, Day of the Dead, and All Souls' Day

The modern holiday of Halloween has its origins in the ancient Celtic festival known as Samhain (pronounced *"sow-in"*) which literally means "summer's end." This festival was a celebration for the end of the harvest season and sometimes referred to as the "Celtic New Year." It was a time used to take stock of supplies and slaughter livestock for the upcoming winter. It was believed that on October 31, the boundaries between the living and the deceased would merge, and the dead would become dangerous for the living by causing problems such as sickness or damaging crops. Frequently, the festivals would involve bonfires along with costumes and masks in an attempt to imitate the evil spirits or appease them. The bonfires were also an attempt to appease the spirits by giving them a place to warm themselves and to light the way for their trip back among the living. Halloween is a shortened version of All Hallows' Day, which is also known as All Saints' Day. Pope Gregory IV in 835 A.D. moved the old Christian Feast of All Saints' Day from May 13, which had been the date of another pagan holiday, the Feast of the Lemures or Lemuria (feast during which the ancient Romans performed ceremonies to remove the malevolent and fearful ghosts of the dead from their homes) to November 1.

The carved pumpkin with a lit candle inside (jack-o'-lantern) is one of the most prominent symbols of Halloween. The tradition may have come from the ancient Celts who placed their ancestors' skulls outside their homes or dwellings during this festival time. The ancient Celts believed the soul resides in the skull, and to keep their loved ones' skulls close by was a way to honor the deceased. Placing the skulls outside their front door was a way to invite their ancestors back home during this hallowed time of year.

Halloween, perceived as the night during which the division between the world of the living and the otherworld was blurred, allowed spirits of the dead and inhabitants from the underworld to walk freely on Earth. Irish and Scottish immigrants brought versions of this festival to North America in the 19th Century. They thought it necessary to dress as a spirit or otherworldly creature when venturing outdoors to blend in, and so began the tradition of Halloween costumes. This gradually evolved into trick-or-treating, as children would knock on their neighbors' doors in order to gather fruit, nuts, and sweets for the world of the living. Salt, used for protection, was sprinkled in the hair of the children to guard them against the evil spirits.

The sinister imagery surrounding Halloween is largely due to the movie industry of Hollywood and graphic artists, by commercializing on dark and mysterious images. Common Halloween characters include ghosts, witches, vampires, bats, zombies, black cats, aliens, skeletons, demons, etc. The colors black and orange are the traditional colors of Halloween. Black is used for symbolizing death, night, witches, black cats, bats, and vampires, and orange is used for symbolizing pumpkins, Autumn, the turning leaves, fires, etc.

All Saints' Day, November 1, is a day all saints known and unknown are honored. All Souls' Day or Day of the Dead is celebrated on November 2. On Day of the Dead Eve, families stay up late and little "soul cakes" are eaten by everyone. At the stroke of midnight, there is silence among the household, as candles burn in every room to guide the souls back to visit their earthly homes. Drinks and food are placed on tables or alter in the main room of the home, as an offering to refresh these souls during their journey. Some celebrations are held at the gravesite of the deceased loved ones.

HAPPY BIRTHDAY

Years ago, people believed evil spirits would cause harm to humans and they thought that these spirits were thought to gather around a person, especially during their birthday celebration. Friends and relatives would gather around the birthday celebrant on their special day to protect them against the unknown dangers that their birthday may hold. This gathering, or party, with its gifts and good wishes was meant to keep the birthday person safe from evil and to insure a good year to come. At first, only kings or prominent men were the only ones important enough to celebrate birthdays. However, as time wore on, the ordinary people began to celebrate their birthdays as well, which eventually led to children's birthdays being celebrated most of all.

Birthday Candles: The early Greeks and Romans thought candles were magical, and would offer their prayers or wishes, which were carried to the Gods/Goddesses through the flames and smoke of the candles. Their hope was that the Gods/Goddesses would answer the prayers, grant the wishes, and send down their blessings due to the use of the candles during the ceremony. The Germans were the first to use candles on birthday cakes, and later, the custom evolved to having one candle to represent each year of life, with an extra one added "to grow on." All of this developed into the custom of having the birthday celebrant make a secret wish on the lit candles. By blowing them out in one puff, in the hopes that the wish, sent via the rising smoke, will reach God/Universe to be granted.

Birthday Games: Playing games at birthday parties started as a symbolic way of erasing the past year with the beginning of a new year. Games that required skill or strength are played to show how much progress the birthday child had made since the previous year. This made the birthday celebrant proud to show how much stronger and/or wiser she had become and also to see how much more she would need to learn to become an adult.

Birthday Spanks: Birthday spanks are given to make sure the birthday celebrate has good luck for the coming year. The spanks, slaps, pinches, hitting, were/are a form of ridding the celebrant of built up negative energy to make way for the good to come in, a form of good luck. But, with much appreciation, this unhealthy practice is not as popular in the 21st Century.

Other Birth Practices: There was a German custom of planting a tree at the time of a child's birth (called a "birth tree"). This practice was in honor of the birth, which gave it a mysterious connection with the child's welfare or life. If the tree flourished and grew strong, the child would have good fortune. However, if the tree was cut down, withered, or died, the child would or/may have a difficult life due to this occurrence.

Astrologers and numerologists use the date, hour, and place of birth to tell what kind of life a person may lead and give insight to that person's personality if born in a certain month at a certain time. Astrology and numerology charts are drawn up to inform the person of lucky days and lucky numbers, or which person under a particular Zodiac sign is compatible as a mate, etc.

A stone, called "birthstone" is associated with each month of the year. Many people believe that if the person who was born in that particular month wears the birthstone, the stone will bring good luck to the wearer. *See* Birthstones in this book for more information.

The book *The Crystal Bible* by Judy Hall is a good source to read up on these particular stones and their special attributes for the person wearing the stone.

HERBS AND HOW TO PRESERVE THEM

These tips may be applied to both cooking with herbs and using them as incense. The shelf life of many herbs is one to two years, but this period is shorter when herbs are exposed to light, heat, and open air. Herb leaves keep their flavor best when they are stored whole, and crushed just before use. When herb seeds are to be used for cooking, the seeds should be stored whole, and ground up as needed.

Bag Drying: To prepare herbs for drying, remove blossoms from the herbs and rinse the leaves on the stem in cold water to remove soil. Allow the herbs to drain on absorbent towels until dry. Then, place the herbs in a paper bag and tie the stems. Leave one to two inches of the stems exposed. This allows the herbs' oil to flow from the stems to the leaves. Place the bag in a warm, dry location. In about one to two weeks, when the leaves become brittle, tap them free of the stems, the leaves will fall into the bag. Store the herbal leaves in an airtight container away from the light. Keep the stems to burn on incense charcoal, to light candles, or fire in the fireplace.

Tray Drying: Clean herbs the same as for bag drying. Put stems and leaves, one layer deep, on a tray in a dark, ventilated room. Turn over the herbs occasionally for uniform drying. The leaves are ready for storage when they are dry and the stems are tough. Keep the stems to burn on incense charcoal, to light candles, or fire in the fireplace.

Freezing Flavor: Herbs may also be frozen. Rinse herbs in cold water and blanch in boiling, unsalted water for 50 seconds. Cool quickly in ice water, package, and freeze. Dill, parsley, chives, and basil may be frozen without blanching.

IMBOLC

Pronounced *"im'olk,"* which means "in the belly," referring to the pregnancy of ewes, Imbolc is a Celtic term for Spring. Imbolc, celebrated February 2, has rituals involving outdoor bonfires or hearth fires, or the use of many candles—representing the return of light/sunlight—in the homes. The special foods prepared during this celebration represent and honor the new crops that are to come. It is a time to prepare for the new planting season and to honor Mother Earth. Cows and ewes are pregnant again, which means the return of milk and cheese.

It is a cross-quarter day on the solar calendar, halfway between the Winter Solstice and Spring Equinox. It is a day dedicated to the Goddess Brigid, also known as St. Brigid's Day, or Candlemas.

It was a time of weather divination. The old tradition of watching to see if snakes, badgers, or other animals would venture out of their winter burrow or den eventually became Groundhog Day in the States.

See Goddess Brigid or Candlemas in this book for more information about Imbolc celebrations.

INCENSE

Burning dried herbs to release their fragrances is perhaps one of the earliest healing rituals known to man. Considered a gift to the Gods, the aromatic smoke was sent with prayers and offerings as it rose up towards the heavens. Burning herbs/incenses was regarded as a disinfectant; they were used in crowded temples to keep the danger of many infectious diseases away.

As with essential oils, incense draws upon the healing components contained in the dried herbs to help calm the mind, relax the body, and soothe the soul. While the effects of incense often vary depending on the herb or combination of herbs used, the power of burning incense has endured over the centuries.

Burning incense in your home: The pleasure of incense is readily available with a minimum of requirements. You will need a fireproof incense burner or bowl to use with ready-made incense sticks or cones, and incense charcoal that is used with such ingredients as herbal leaves, berries, root powders, and petals. All of these may be purchased at most health food or metaphysical stores.

How to burn incense on charcoal: Follow these steps to ensure the proper use of incense and to maximize its effects. Sprinkle a small handful of sand into an incense bowl, which will provide sufficient ventilation for the charcoal to burn. Next, place one or two incense charcoals on top of the sand and light with a match. Arrange the incense on top of the charcoal, making sure to use only a pinch of homemade blend (or prepared blend from the store). As the incense begins to burn, use a hand-held fan, feather, or your hand to move air towards it to stoke the fire and distribute the smoke. Use pliers to rearrange the embers.

The charcoal and sand in your incense burner or bowl needs to be removed after each use. Before discarding, be certain that there are no live embers in the ashes.

Lean how to create your own incense by visiting the internet, your local metaphysical/health food shop, or bookstore.

LAMMAS
Also called Lughnasadh (pronounced "Loo-NAS-a")

Lammas is celebrated on August 1 and is one of the cross-quarters of the year. It is a festival that marks the end of Summer and the beginning of Fall or Autumn. The ancient Celts called it Lughnasadh, named after their Sun God Lugh. As the days begin to grow shorter after the Summer Solstice, Lammas is a festival that honors the harvesting of the grain for the coming winter. Ceremonially, the first bundle of wheat or oats gathered were milled and baked into loaves of bread to be consumed during the Lammas festivities. This was done to give homage to the grain for its death, so that the people or village would survive the coming cold winter. By eating this bread, the bread of the Gods/Goddesses (givers of life), it is reminiscent of the Christian Lord's Supper or Communion with the bread being blessed, and used to represent the body of Christ/God, then consumed to nourish the Christian believers.

In celebrating Lammas or Lughnasadh in today's time, it is a great way to honor our ancestors and to give thanks for the abundance we have in our lives. Additionally, it is a way to be grateful for the food on our tables and to show respect for the hard work our ancestors went through in order to survive. It is also a time for us to make note of the fruition of our New Year's resolutions and to make adjustments, if necessary. Or, to contemplate new resolutions for the upcoming New Year. Lammas is a time that represents change, renewal, and new development in our lives.

MABON OR FALL/AUTUMN EQUINOX

Mabon is celebrated on the Fall or Autumn Equinox, which in the northern hemisphere occurs on September 21 or 22. Mabon is also the crone phase of the Triple Goddess—things are coming to an end. The Fall Equinox is celebrated as a thanksgiving to honor Mother Earth by giving thanks for the blessings we have received throughout the year to honor Her for providing for us during the upcoming winter months.

Mabon is one of the eight Wiccan Sabbats, it is the second of the three harvest festivals, preceded by Lammas and followed by Samhain. Mabon or Fall Equinox is a time to prepare for the winter ahead; to become accustomed to the shorter days, longer nights. It is a good time to perform magical spells for protection, wealth and prosperity, self-confidence, balance and harmony, and setting goals.

MAY DAY, BELTANE, OR FIRST DAY OF SUMMER

The May Day festival began in ancient Rome in honor of Flora, the Goddess of flowers and springtime. Later, this festival spread to other lands conquered by the Romans. It reached its height in England during the Middle Ages. On May Day, the villagers would rise at dawn to go "a-maying." They would roam the countryside gathering blossoming flowers and branches to decorate their homes. Flowers were woven into wreaths or garlands to exchange as gifts between lovers or to hang on doors as decorations. Or, flowers were placed in baskets and left on doorsteps for the recipients to find in the morning. Hawthorn is known for being lucky and favorable because it begins to bloom when the weather is warm enough for planting. Anyone who went out into the woods and found a branch of flowering hawthorn (also called "may") would bring it triumphantly back to the village (thereby bringing in the May) and announce the start of the planting season. However, there were warnings about bringing hawthorn into the house, as it would also invited in the fairies. As they were, known to be the mischievous and love playing pranks on humans.

The villagers would erect a towering maypole on the village green. This pole was decorated with bright flowers, fruits, and streamers. The villagers would then dance and sing around the maypole, sometimes accompanied by a piper. Maypoles were usually set up just for the day in small towns, but in larger towns they were erected permanently. In some larger towns, children would go from house to house handing out flowers in return for pennies. After the pennies were collected, the children would throw them into a wishing well in hopes that their wishes would be granted. The pennies were later collected and given to the poor.

May Day, also called "Beltane" (Bright Fire) by the ancient Celts, considered the first day of summer, and a time when the veil between worlds are opened. Beltane is the time of milk and honey. The bees are busy pollinating the new crops and plants. With the return of honey to make their meads and sweeten their meals, and the abundance of milk and cheese, it is a symbol that cows and bees are very important during this time of year. The villagers had made it through the long cold winter and it is time to celebrate and honor the return of the better things in life.

Before returning the cows to pasture, they were blessed in protection rituals to keep their milk from souring by running them through the embers and smoke of the bonfires. In times past, sacrifices were offered that included human beings. Large oatcakes, called bannocks, were eaten as part of the festivities. Traditionally, a portion of the cake was burned or marked with ashes. The unfortunate soul who received the marked piece was sacrificed to the Gods. More recently, the recipient jumps over a small fire three times instead, with the height of the leap used to forecast the height of the crops. Beltane celebrated love, attraction, courtship, and mating—that yearly build-up of desire we refer to as "spring fever." Long before our current high school prom king and queen, villages elected a young, attractive couple to represent the King and Queen of the May. The villagers would dance around the May pole—a phallic symbol, and enjoy other May Day festivities with some of the celebrants spending the night together under the stars in the forest. It is said that children conceived during this magical time would have the "second sight" (a seer), and the power and skills of all creatures.

The Puritans frowned on May Day and brought this attitude with them to the New World, as it has never been celebrated here in the U.S. with as much enthusiasm as in Great Britain or other parts of the world.

May Day wine is made by flavoring wine with herbs, berries, fruits, or flowers. The traditional May Day wine is white wine flavored with sweet woodruff (an herb). Pick sweet woodruff whose blossoms have not yet opened the day before you want to serve the wine, as the herb has more flavor if slightly dried. Tie the stems of a bunch of the herb with cotton thread and hang it in a bottle of wine so the leaves are covered. After ten or fifteen minutes, remove the woodruff. Some recipes for May Day wine tell you to leave the woodruff in the wine for days, even weeks. However, woodruff contains *coumarin*, a substance similar to Coumadin, which is prescribed to thin blood for people suffering from clots. However, too much woodruff can cause headaches, so it is best to use only enough to flavor the wine. If you don't drink alcohol, woodruff can also be used in the same way to flavor milk or apple juice. Drink a toast to the glory of May and you might also want to use this wine in a love ritual.

MOON PHASES

Waxing Moon is when She grows from new (dark) to full. The New Moon provides the correct amount of energy for constructing magical workings requiring growth, enhancement, or improvement. It is a good time for new beginnings, new love, building businesses, friendships, partnerships, finding a new job, and financial prosperity. It also provides ideal conditions for planting herbs, developing your psyche, and for your health/well-being/vitality. The Goddess aspect of the waxing moon is maiden.

Full Moon has three days of expression, the day before, the day of, and the day after. Nevertheless, Her energy is most intense when She reaches complete fullness. Any magical effort, especially difficult ones, can benefit greatly from the potency of this phase. Use the Full Moon to amplify magical intent and to give magical workings additional power. The Goddess aspect of the full moon is mother.

Waning Moon is when She decreases from full to new. In this phase, She offers energy suitable for banishing or releasing the old, removing unwanted negative energies, and reversing circumstances. This phase may be used to end undesirable eating patterns, break bad habits, or to remove yourself from dysfunctional partnerships or stressful situations. The Goddess aspect of the waning moon is crone.

New Moon or Dark Moon may be used as a period of rest, relaxation, and regeneration. However, magical workings may be done for starting new ventures, new beginnings, love/romance, enhancing psychic powers, and divination. Workings during the New Moon are done on the day of, to three-and-a-half days after. The Goddess aspect of the new moon is re-birth.

Blue Moon occurs when there are two full moons in one month, which happens approx. every three years. The second full moon is called a blue moon, hence the term "Once in a Blue Moon." A blue moon happens during Halloween once every 80 years. Use the second full moon (blue moon) in any calendar month to set long-term goals and implement exciting new changes. The power of the moon on earth and in our lives is enhanced and doubled during the occurrence of the Blue Moon.

Black Moon occurs when there are two new moons in one month, but this term is not as well known or frequently used as is Blue Moon. It is said that the second new moon or black moon is a time of great power within the spiritual and magical world, and any workings during this time are especially powerful.

There are two types of eclipses: Solar Eclipse, which occurs during the New Moon phase, with the Moon passing directly between the Earth and the Sun. A Lunar Eclipse happens when the Moon darkens as it passes into the Earth's shadow. Many believe that an eclipse signals a change and can act as a turning point in their lives. The solar eclipse affects the external and the lunar eclipse affects the personal or internal, such as emotions.

The trick to working with an eclipse: buy an almanac to know the date and time for when the eclipse will take place; plan ahead to know precisely what you would like to change in your life; and begin your magical workings ten minutes before the eclipse is to occur. Continue your spell casting throughout the eclipse until you are completely finished. The idea is to harness the energy of the eclipse as it builds and to draw down the energy to you for your workings. If the eclipse is not visible in your part of the world, no worries here, as the intent of your workings are present and the energy of the eclipse is felt no matter if the eclipse is visible to you or not. The energy of the eclipse will merge with your workings to produce the outcome you seek.

A simple and effective way to use the power of the moon: Write out what you want to release on one piece of paper, then write out what you want to attract/manifest on another piece of paper. Sit outside, if possible, during the full moon and meditate on your request(s) for a few minutes. Burn the pieces of paper one at time, take a few minutes between each burning, and reflect on what you have written down as it is burning and release your request to the Universe/Spirit. Do not dwell on what you have released and/or wish to manifest again, just trust that the Universe/Spirit is taking care of everything and that all is as it should be at this point or time of your life.

THE MORRIGAN

The Morrigan is the shape-shifting Celtic Goddess of War, Fate, and Death. She is also a Goddess of the rivers, lakes, revenge, night, magic, prophecy, priestesses, and witches. She is also a Triple Goddess. She watches over battlefields in the form of a raven or crow and influences the outcome of a battle. Her role in Celtic legend is similar to that of the Valkyries in Norse folklore.

Another guise of the Morrigan is that of the "Washer at the Ford." The washer is the one washing the blood spotted clothes of past warriors. The warrior who sees her before a battle knows his time is up and that he would be next to die in battle. The Morrigan is an appropriate deity for strong, independent people, particularly those on a warrior's path[9].

---

9 A warrior's path: A decision to embark on a path of self-discovery and self-healing is the mark of a great warrior or master. As this spiritual warrior is willing or has the courage to face their own darkness, demons, and their inner selves to see or be the change that their spiritual path requires.

In one legend concerning the Morrigan, she appears to the hero Cuchulainn (son of the God Lugh) and offers her love to him. When he fails to recognize her and rejects her, the Morrigan, deeply wounded, informs Cuchulainn that she will hinder him while he is in battle. When Cuchulainn finally perishes, she settles on his shoulder in the form of a raven. His misfortune was that he never realized the feminine power of sovereignty or control that the Morrigan offered to him. She appeared to him on at least four occasions and each time he failed to recognize her.

Mythical Creatures

- **Banshee** or Bean Sidhe is from Irish *bean sí*—woman of the faery mounds. She is a female spirit from Irish mythology seen as an omen of death and a messenger from the Otherworld. According to legend, a banshee wails or keens around a house or dwelling if someone in the house is about to die. Banshees are usually dressed in white or grey, and often have long, fair hair, which they brush with a silver comb. Her Scottish counterpart is the *bean nighe*—washerwoman. Sidhe means "fairy mounds" and is pronounced as *"shee"* which is often incorrectly used for both the mounds and people of the mounds. The people of the mounds are the faeries or fairies.

- **Brownies** inhabit houses and aid in tasks around the house. However, they do not like to be seen and will only work at night, traditionally in exchange for small gifts or food. They usually abandon the house if their gifts are called "payments," or if the owners of the house misuse them. Brownies make their homes in an unused part of the house. They are also the guardians of dragons.

- **Centaurs:** In Greek mythology, they are a race of creatures composed of part human and part horse. Centaurs are notorious for being overly indulgent drinkers and carousers, given to violence when intoxicated, and generally uncultured.

◈ **Cyclops** is a giant with a single eye in the middle of its forehead and has a foul disposition. The name Cyclops is a synonym for brute-strength and power, and they are known for their well-crafted weapons.

◈ **Dragons** are sometimes described as huge, fire-breathing, scaly, horned dinosaur-like creatures, with leathery wings, four legs, and a long muscular tail. Or, they are sometimes shown with feathered wings, fiery manes, and various exotic colorations. Asian dragons, a symbol for the Chinese emperors, usually are long serpent-like creatures which have the scales of a fish, horns of a deer, feet of an eagle, the body of a snake, a feathery mane, large eyes, and may be holding a pearl to control lightning. Dragons are bringers of rain, live in, and govern bodies of water (e.g., lakes, rivers, oceans, seas, or wells). Asian dragons are benevolent, yet bossy, but western dragons are portrayed as malevolent. Many ancient European stories of dragons have them guarding a hoard of ancient treasure. The treasure is always cursed and ill will is brought to those who later possess it. Dragons often have major spiritual significance in various religions and cultures around the world. In many Eastern and Native American cultures, dragons are revered as representatives of the primal forces of nature and the universe, and represent wisdom. *See* Ouroboros in this section.

◈ **Dwarf** is a short, stocky humanoid creature in Norse mythology, as well as Germanic mythologies, fairy tales, fantasy fiction, and role-playing games. In mythology, Dwarves are much like humans, but generally prefer to live underground or in mountainous areas. They are known to have treasures of gold, silver, and precious stones, and pass their time in producing valuable weapons and armor. They are well known for their mining and smith work. Generally shorter than humans, they are stockier and hairier, usually sporting full beards. Though slow runners and poor riders, dwarves are excellent warriors.

◈ **Elf** is a creature of Germanic and Norse folklore. The elves were originally a race of minor nature and fertility Gods/Goddesses, often pictured as youthful men and women of great beauty, living in forests and underground places, or in wells and springs. They ae long-lived and have magical powers. Crossbreeding was consequently possible between elves and humans in the Old Norse belief. Elves are typically pictured as fair-haired, white-clad, and can be spiteful when offended. One can appease the elves by offering them a treat, preferably butter. In addition to these human aspects, they are commonly described as semi-divine beings associated with fertility. Like spirits, the elves are not bound by physical limitations and can pass through walls and doors, as in the manner of ghosts. If a human encounters elves and becomes involved in their celebrations, the human will discover that even though only a few hours seemed to have passed in elfin time, many years have passed in human years.

◈ **Fairy** (fey or fae or faery; collectively wee folk, good folk, people of peace, or hidden ones) is a Celtic metaphysical spirit or supernatural being, and is similar to an Elf in Norse folklore. Fairies or Faeries are generally portrayed as human in appearance and as having supernatural abilities such as the ability to fly, cast spells, and to influence or foresee the future. In modern culture, they are portrayed as young, winged, females of small stature. Wings, while common in modern artwork, were rare in folktales of old. These tales told how fairies flew with magic, or sometimes flew on ragwort (ragweed) stems, or on the backs of birds, but the tales never mentioned wings.

- Some beliefs are that fairies are the dead, or some sub-class of the dead. Another belief is when the angels revolted, God ordered the gates shut; those still in heaven remained angels, while those in hell became devils, and those caught in between became fairies. Another theory is that a race of small people who once lived in the Celtic lands and British Isles were driven into hiding by invading humans. They came to be seen as another race, or possibly spirits, and were believed to live in the Otherworld, or it was said they existed by living underground, in hidden hills, or ancient burial mounds (faery or fairy mounds).

- The fairies' fear of iron was attributed to the invading races having iron weapons, whereas they only had flint arrowheads (elf-shot) and were, therefore, easily defeated in physical battle. Their green clothing and underground homes are due to their need of camouflaging themselves from hostile humans, and their use of magic is seen as a necessary skill for combating those with superior weaponry.

- Faeries are noted for their mischief and malice. Some of their pranks may be tangling the hair of sleepers into "Elf-locks," stealing small items, or leading a traveler astray. However, in times past, the faeries were blamed for more harmful actions such as causing consumption (tuberculosis) by forcing young men and women to attend dances (revels) every night, causing them to waste away from lack of rest. Or, fairies riding domestic animals at night, such as cows, could cause paralysis or mysterious illnesses of the animals. However, other things were regarded as unfavorable to the fairies like wearing clothing inside out, running water, bells (especially church bells or cowbells), St. John's Wort, and four-leaf clovers are just a few. *Example:* To keep the cows' milk from spoiling, cowbells, which are made of iron, were hung around their necks to discourage the faeries' mischief.

- A common feature of the fairies is the use of magic to disguise their appearance. Faery gold is notoriously unreliable, appearing as gold when paid, but soon, thereafter, it becomes leaves, flower blossoms, gingerbread cakes, or a variety of other useless things.

◈ **Familiar:** A familiar serves its owners as domestic servants, farmhands, spies, and companions, in addition to helping bewitch enemies. These spirits also inspire artists and writers (a muse). The most common species identified as familiars are cats (particularly black cats), owls, dogs, and sometimes, ferrets, mice, frogs, toads, crows, or hares.

◈ **Faun:** Fauns are spirits of Roman mythology. Fauns are guardian spirits who can grant intellectual powers. Usually they guarded the forests/woodlands. They are known as drunken followers of Bacchus. Bacchus is the God of Wine and the inspirer of ritual madness and ecstasy. Fauns resemble humans above the waist and goats below.

◈ **Feeorin:** In Celtic folklore, Feeorin is a term for fairies who are friendly or at least neutral towards humans. They are small people, either having green skin or are clothed in green, wearing red caps. They enjoy singing and dancing.

◈ **Gargoyle:** In architecture, gargoyles are the carved terminations to spouts, which convey water away from the sides of buildings. Statues representing gargoyle-like creatures are popular sales items, particularly in Goth and New Age retail stores. The gargoyle's grotesque form is said to scare off evil spirits. They are used for protection and are said to come alive at night to watch over the building they are stationed on. Gargoyles are a winged humanoid race with demonic features: horns, a tail, and talons. They are able to turn into stone when necessary.

❖ **Genie/Jinni/Ginni:** Genie came from Latin genius, which means a sort of guardian spirit, assigned to each person at birth. The word genie is the translation of jinni used in the book *The Book of One Thousand and One Arabian Nights*, by Geraldine McCaughrean. In pre-Islamic Arabian mythology and in Islam, a jinni is a member of the jinn, a race of supernatural creatures. The word "jinn" literally means anything which has the connotation of concealment, invisibility, seclusion, and remoteness, and is sometimes associated with succubi (demons in the form of beautiful women). The jinn have communities much like human societies: they eat, marry, have very long lives (2,500 years), die, etc. They are invisible to humans, but they are able to see humans. A jinni is able to take on any physical form, which may be human, animal, nature, etc. One of the activities associated with a jinni is fortune telling. They are mischievous and enjoy punishing humans, which caused humans to associate accidents and diseases to the jinn. Sometimes, a jinni can be tricked and bound to a talisman—a lamp, bottle with a stopper, ring, etc. and when released they must grant three wishes or requests. If the person (the master) does not make the final wish, the jinni remains bound to the talisman and master. However, once the third wish is granted, the jinni is released from the talisman and servitude.

❖ **Ghost** is an apparition of a deceased person who hangs around places or people, possibly not knowing that they are dead. They may be looking for closure or revenge, or they may be afraid to crossover to the other side. Some are harmless, but others can be very mischievous and evil.

❖ **Ghoul** (ghul) is a monster from ancient Arabian folklore that dwell in burial grounds and other uninhabited places where they rob graves and eat the newly buried dead. Ghuls also hang out in the desert and are shape-shifting demons that usually take on the appearance of a hyena. Also, they slay and devour travelers of the deserts.

◈ **Giant:** Giants are human in appearance, but just on a much, much larger scale. They often cause chaos wherever they happen to be. Moreover, with having wild, uncontrollable natures, they often fought with the Gods, according to Greek and Norse mythology. Giants are mentioned in the Old Testament, with the most famous one being Goliath. They have superhuman strength, long lifespan; with some of them possess a great deal of knowledge as well. In some folklore, they built the remains of earlier civilizations. Giants were the ones who they used to explain the large constructed monuments, buildings, walls, and some of the naturally formed structures such as Giant's Causeway in Northern Ireland. Some of our fairy tales have given us the perception of giants as stupid and violent monsters, frequently said to eat humans, especially children. Hagrid of *Harry Potter* series by J.K. Rowling has given us a different image of giants.

◈ **Gnomes** are the elementals for Earth and described as gnarled old men, who live underground and guard buried treasure. Their king, Gob, ruled over them with a magical sword. In fantasy games such as Dungeons & Dragons, they are good-natured, magical beings with a high level of intelligence. They are curious creatures that have poor judgment. In the *Harry Potter* series by J.K. Rowling, gnomes are garden pests and appear to be more like small animals than intelligent beings.

◈ **Goblin** is a general term meant to describe any small mischievous being, grotesquely disfigured, and the size of a dwarf or small human. The word goblin come from Gob or Ghob, the king of the gnomes, whose minions were called Ghob-lings. Also, a creature that resembles a goblin, but larger than a human, is sometimes referred to as an "Ogre" or "Troll."

◈ **Gorgon:** In Greek mythology, the Gorgon is a vicious female monster with sharp fangs and hair of living, venomous snakes. She is a protective deity whose power is so strong that those (especially men) who looked upon her immediately turned to stone. Her image is upon the outside of buildings and dwellings, and placed on containers of wine for protection. *See* Medusa in this section.

❖ **Gremlins** are mischievous creatures that have a specific interest in sabotaging aircraft. Their myth originated among aviators during WWII. The pilots blamed gremlins for sabotaging their aircraft when things went wrong. They are also blamed when things go wrong with motorcycles, which is why some owners hang a small "gremlin" bell on their bike to keep the creatures away. In the 1984 movie *Gremlins* and its 1990 sequel *Gremlins 2: The New Batch*, they obviously have nothing to do with aircraft, though they were portrayed as sabotaging mechanical things. Gremlins also appear in Dungeons & Dragons as miniature humanoid monsters with varying degrees of motivation to cause mayhem and mischief.

❖ **Griffin** or gryphon is a creature with the body of a lion and the head and wings of an eagle. With the lion considered the king of the beasts, and the eagle the king of the birds, the griffin is a remarkably powerful and majestic creature. The griffin is a symbol of divine power and with its image placed upon buildings, dwellings, coins, etc., it is seen as guarding the treasures and protection of the inhabitants within such dwellings. Some illustrations show the griffin with the forelegs of an eagle and lion hindquarters.

❖ **Grim Reaper** is the personification of death as a living, sentient entity and is a concept that has existed in many societies since the beginning of recorded history. In Western cultures, death is usually given the name "The Grim Reaper" and shown as a skeletal figure carrying a large scythe, wearing a midnight-black hooded cloak. Usually, when portrayed in the hooded cloak, only the eyes are seen. The Grim Reaper is, sometimes referred to as the "Angel of Death."

◈ **Hag** or crone is a wizened old woman, witch, Goddess, or a fairy often found in folklore and children's tales such as *Hansel and Gretel*. Hags are often seen as malevolent, and being one of the chosen forms of shape-shifting deities. Many stories about hags are used to frighten children into being good. Small stones with holes in them are magical and are called "Hag Stones" or "Witch Stones." They are used as protective talismans to ward off evil, protect against eye diseases, and discourage nightmares.

◈ **Halcyon** is the name of a bird in Greek legend that is associated with the kingfisher. The halcyon is said to calm the surface of the sea for fourteen days in order to brood her eggs on a floating nest at the time around the Winter Solstice—usually the 21st or 22nd of December. The Halcyon Days are said to begin on the 14th or 15th of December. Halcyon means calm, tranquil, happy, or carefree and is referred to as "Halcyon Days." Our current use of halcyon days tends to be nostalgic in recalling the seemingly endless sunny days of youth.

◈ **Hellhound** is a demonic dog of Hell and typically has features such as being unnaturally large and having three heads. It has black fur, glowing eyes, super strength, and speed; and sometimes has the ability to talk. The hellhound often guards the entrance to the world of the dead, hunts down lost souls, or guards a supernatural treasure. Hagid's dog, Fluffy, was used to guard the Philosopher's Stone in the *Harry Potter* series by J.K. Rowling.

◈ **Hippogriff**, also spelled Hippogryph, is the offspring of a griffin and a mare. They are a rarity, as griffins regard horses as prey. They are a symbol for impossibility and love because they would not exist otherwise. The hippogriff is easier to tame than a griffin and is usually the pet of a knight or a sorcerer, making it an excellent mount, as it has the ability to fly as fast as lightning. The hippogriff is said to be an omnivore, eating either plants or meat. Hagrid had a pet hippogriff named Buckbeak in the *Harry Potter* series by J.K. Rowling.

◈ **Hobbits**, according to J.R.R. Tolkien, live in the lands of Middle-earth, and known as "Halflings." They are very fond of having uneventful lives that are filled with farming, eating, and socializing. Hobbit is a word derived from the name "Holbytlan," which means "hole-dwellers," as their homes are usually dug into the hillsides. The most familiar hobbits are Frodo Baggins, Samwise Gamgee, Peregrin Took, and Meridoc Brandbuck. To find out more, refer to J.R.R. Tolkien's series: *The Hobbit, The Fellowship of the Ring, The Two Towers,* and *The Return of the King.*

◈ **Hobgoblin** was a term used for a friendly or amusing goblin. However, the name is sometimes interchangeable with boogeyman or bugaboo, and these terms are used to frighten children into being good, such as: "You need to stay in bed or the boogeyman will get you."

◈ **Imps** are mischievous, threatening supernatural beings. This Middle Age term was used for any spirits that served witches. They are similar to goblins or gremlins.

◈ **Incubus** (plural incubi) is a demon in male form that preys upon women. The incubus drains energy from the woman on whom it performs sexual acts in order to sustain itself and to impregnate her in order to produce more incubi. Usually the woman expires after giving birth, and so the hunt begins again for the incubus to continue the propagation of more incubi.

◈ **Knockers** or Tommyknockers are the Welsh and Cornish equivalent of leprechauns or brownies. They are beings who are about two feet in height, that live underground, and are skilled in the arts of mining and tunneling where they are known to cause mischief, such as stealing tools and food from miners. Their name comes from the knocking on the mine walls that happens just before cave-ins. According to Cornish folklore, the Knockers are the helpful spirits of miners who had perished in previous accidents in the tin mines. The knocking noise is a warning to the miners of impending danger and for them to seek safety. The miners give thanks and honor the Knockers for the warnings by leaving bits of bread or pastries in the mines.

◈ **Leprechauns** are aged, diminutive men who are frequently found in an intoxicated state, caused by their home-brewed poteen. They love playing pranks on humans as they regard humans as being foolish and greedy. They are known for their wealth, cobbler skills, and for the love of shoes. Supposedly, if you can find the end of a rainbow, you will find a pot of gold, a leprechaun's pot of gold that is.

◈ **Medusa:** In Greek mythology, Medusa is a monstrous, underworld female character, that when gazed upon, turns the onlookers (especially men) to stone. Medusa is also tripled into a trio of sisters, the Gorgons—Medusa, Stheno, and Euryale. She is a beautiful nymph who was raped by Poseidon in Athena's temple. The Goddess Athena, who is very jealous of Medusa and her beauty, transforms Medusa's beautiful hair to serpents, her face becomes so terrible to behold that the mere sight of it turns a man to stone. *See* Gorgon in this section.

◈ **Mermaid** is a aquatic creature with the head and torso of a human female and the tail of a fish. The male version of a mermaid is called a merman; the gender-neutral plural is merfolk or merpeople. Mermaids, sometimes compared to sirens, would sing to sailors to enchant them, distracting them from their work and cause them to walk off the ship's deck, or cause shipwrecks. Forgetting that humans are not able to breathe underwater, the sailors would drown as the mermaids attempted to take them down to their underwater kingdoms. Mermaids would sometimes warn the ships of impending bad weather on the horizon. Beach glass is said to be the tears of mermaids that are shed for the love of the sailor(s) who is lost at sea due to the many bad storms. So, remember that the next time you find the sand-polished, shards of glass upon the beach to treasure your find knowing it is made with the love of a mermaid.

❖ **Merrow** is the Scottish and Irish Gaelic term for mermaid and mermen. The merrow-maidens, like mermaids, would lure human males to join them in their magical watery kingdom, where the humans were able to exist in an enchanted state. The females were also said to have a red cap or cape, and if a human male was able to get the red cap or cape and hide it from her, the female merrow would stay with the human, raise a family, and live a happy life. However, if she came upon her red cape, she would be compelled to return to the sea, leaving her human loved ones behind.

❖ **Minotaur:** In Greek mythology, the Minotaur is a creature that is part man and part bull. The Minotaur caused such terror and destruction on Crete that Minos (legendary king of Crete and son of Zeus) summoned Daedalus (famous architect) to build a gigantic, intricate labyrinth that would be impossible for the Minotaur to escape. Every nine years, Athens sent seven of their finest young men and young maidens to Crete, as a sacrifice to the Minotaur, where they are locked in the labyrinth for the Minotaur to feast upon. When the hero Theseus heard of this practice, he went to Crete, killed the Minotaur, thus releasing Athens of this gory duty.

❖ **Muse:** In Greek mythology, the Muses are a sisterhood of Goddesses and/or spirits that inspired artistic creation with their inspiration and divine guidance. In this day and time, we refer to an artistic inspiration as to "having found my muse."

❖ **Nymph:** In Greek mythology, a nymph is any member of a large class of female nature entities. They are frequently associated with the superior divinities: the hunter, Artemis; the prophetic, Apollo; the reveler and God of Wine, Dionysus; and Gods such as Pan and Hermes. Nymphs are known to live in groves of trees, by springs/rivers, or in valleys and caves. They could move swiftly and invisibly, ride through the air, and slip through small holes. Although not immortal, they live exceeding long lives and retained their beauty until death. They also accompany Poseidon and are friendly and helpful towards sailors, protecting them during storms.

◈ **Ogre** is a brutal, very strong, hideous, and overly large humanoid monster that feeds on human beings, especially children. In fairy tales, ogres would kidnap the beautiful princess that invariably was rescued by a knight in shining armor. However, we know those knights in shining armor don't really exist.

◈ **Ouroboros** is an ancient symbol of a serpent or dragon swallowing its own tail and forming a circle, referring to unity and infinity, a symbol for the Universe. The ouroboros may also be shown as half-light and half-dark, resembling Yin/Yang, which illustrates the duality of all things and symbolizes that opposites are not necessarily in conflict with each other. In alchemy, the ouroboros symbolizes the circular nature of the alchemist's work, uniting opposites—the conscious and unconscious minds. It is also used to represent the constant re-occurrence of life: birth/life/re-birth, and so on. The Milky Way Galaxy is thought to be an inspiration for this symbol, as it resembles a serpent in the night's sky. There is an ancient myth that refers to a serpent of light residing in the heavens, and this serpent was said to eat its own tail, representing birth/re-birth. *See* Dragons in this section.

◈ **Pegasus:** In Greek mythology, Pegasus is a winged horse who is the son of Poseidon and the Gorgon-Medusa. Athena caught and tamed Pegasus, and presented him to the Muses, who in turn made him serve the poets. Zeus honored Pegasus for his faithful service by transforming him into a constellation. In modern terminology, the word Pegasus has come to refer to any winged horse.

❖ **Phoenix:** Phoenix is the elemental for Fire and lives for over 500 years. The phoenix is a bird with beautiful gold and red plumage, and is a symbol of "death and re-birth." At the end of its life cycle, the phoenix builds itself a nest of cinnamon twigs, which it then ignites. The Phoenix and its nest both burn up into a pile of ashes, from which a new, young phoenix arises. This new phoenix has the same lifespan as the old phoenix. The phoenix is able to regenerate when hurt or wounded; therefore, it does not have to wait until the end of its lifespan. This regeneration process makes the bird almost immortal and invincible. A tear from its eye can heal a person, and make the person temporarily immune to death, as well. *Note:* Cinnamon was highly prized in the ancient world and mostly only used by the monarchy or ruling class. It was used on funeral pyres for love and purification. The Emperor Nero was reported to have burned a year's supply of it at the funeral of his beloved wife.

❖ **Pixies**, usually depicted as wingless, with pointed ears, and often wearing a green outfit, with a pointed hat. Pixies enjoy playing tricks on people, for example, by stealing their belongings or throwing things at them. They love to ride horses and would borrow them during the night, but would return them to the owners before dawn, leaving only tangled manes as evidence of the prank. Pixies also help single moms by doing the housework at night while the household slept, so the moms will have more time to tend to the children and other mundane human activities. As a show of respect, and to placate them, leave small gifts such as bowls of food or saucers of milk out at night, as this might persuade the pixies to help you out with your household chores while you are sleeping.

❖ **Pooka/Puca** is a fairy shape-shifter in animal form. The puca may appear as an eagle, very large rabbit (*see* the movie *Harvey* staring James Stewart), or as a large black goat (its origin with the early Irish "poc" a male goat, which lends its name to Puck, the goat-footed satyr made famous in Shakespeare's *A Midsummer Night's Dream*). It most commonly takes the form of a black or white horse with a flowing mane and glowing yellow eyes. The pooka is, considered by many, to be the most terrifying of all fairy creatures. It interferes with those out at night, by tossing them onto its back and giving them the ride of their lives, which is not necessarily a pleasant one. The Water-horse, a similar creature, will allow itself to be ridden, but if the rider takes it to a body of water (lake/pond/river), the water-horse will take the rider deep into the water and rip him to pieces. The puca is also associated with Samhain/Halloween, when the last of the crops are harvested. Any crop remaining in the fields on Halloween night is considered "pooka" or "fairy-blasted" and thought to be unfit for human consumption. Some farmers will leave a small share of the crop, "puca's share," to appease the creature. November 1 sometimes referred to as "Pooka" or "Puca's Day," the one day of the year when it is expected to behave in an agreeable manner and, if consulted, may give insightful information regarding the consultant's future or of the coming New Year.

◈ **Prometheus** of Greek mythology is the Titan honored for stealing fire from Zeus on the stalk of a fennel plant and giving it to mortals for their use. Zeus ordered him chained on top of the Caucasus (this mountain range is the dividing line between Asia and Europe). Every day an eagle would eat his liver, but since he was an immortal, his liver always grew back. Every day he has to endure this pain. Prometheus is described as an intelligent and cunning man who had sympathy for humanity. The term Promethean is used to refer to events or people of great creativity, intellect, and boldness.

◈ **Satyrs** have the upper half of a man and the lower half of a goat, with a long, thick horsetail. Mature satyrs have goat's horns, while juveniles have bony nubs on their foreheads. They are described as being mischievous, but cowardly. They are lovers of wine and women, and are ready for every physical pleasure. They travel to the music of pipes, cymbals, castanets, and bagpipes, and love to dance with the nymphs, with whom they are obsessed. Satyrs are immortal, but they do grow old.

◈ **Selkie** is a sea creature disguised as a seal who is able to transform to human form by shedding their "seal skin" and are able to revert back to seal form by putting their "selkie skin" back on. Stories concerning selkies are generally romantic tragedies. The human lover hides the selkie's skin, thus preventing it from returning to seal form. However, if the selkie finds their seal skin, they are compelled to return to the sea, leaving their human lover and family behind.

◈ **Shade** is a supernatural creature that takes the shape of a person or animal. It can control shadow movement by darkening a room or sinking into a shadow and appearing out of another shadow in a totally different area. Another supernatural creature such as a vampire, werewolf, or another Shade can only kill a Shade.

◈ **Sirens** are mermaid-like creatures in Greek mythology that lived on an island surrounded by cliffs and rocks. Seamen, lured by the sirens' enchanting music, sailing too close to the island, invariably became shipwrecked on the rocky coast. The term "siren song" refers to an appeal that is hard to resist, and if listened to, will lead to bad results.

◈ **Sprite:** The term sprite is generally used in reference to elf-like creatures, including fairies, dwarves, and various spiritual beings such as ghosts. They do not like being ignored, and tend to leave the person they are troubling because they are not receiving the attention or reaction they have come to expect.

◈ **Succubus** (plural succubi) is the female counterpart of the incubus that preys upon human males. They sleep with the men to collect their sperm, which they give to the incubus who would then use it to impregnate human females, thus explaining how demons were able to spawn children. Such children created this way are more susceptible to the influence of demons or evil spirits. This is how the term "devil's spawn" came about. In the 16th century, the carving of a succubus on the outside of an inn indicated that the establishment also operated as a brothel.

◈ **Sylph** is the elemental for Air and is an invisible being of the air, which is also used as a term for minor spirits (air spirits), elementals, or fairies of the air. Sylphs are sometimes portrayed as mischievous creatures that cause devastating natural disasters, such as storms and tornadoes, when angered. However, they also create beautiful cloud formations with their wings. They also help healing practitioners on their path to enlightenment.

◈ **Thunderbird** is a creature common to Native Americans that often appears on totem poles. The thunderbird's massive wingspan is said to create storms when it flies. Clouds are pulled together by its wing-beats, with its wings making the sound of thunder. It releases bolts of lightning from its eyes when it blinks, and it carries lightning bolts in its talons. Thunderbirds are intelligent, powerful, and wrathful beings. The thunderbird is a servant to the Great Spirit and protects humans by fighting the evil spirits that prey upon the humans.

◈ **Trolls** are a fearsome race from Norse mythology. They live underground in hills, caves, or mounds. The males are regarded as having poor intellect, with the females being quite shrewd. They are mischievous and like playing tricks on humans. Trolls sometimes steal newborn human babies and leave their offspring with the human to raise. These babies or children, called changelings, have a greenish tint to their skin, malicious tempers, and dislike wearing shoes, but they are much wiser and intelligent then human children.

◈ **Undine** is a water nymph or water spirit, and the elemental of Water. The undines usually found in forest pools and waterfalls, and possess beautiful voices. According to some legends, in order for the undine to acquire a soul, she must marry a human male and have his children, thus losing her immortality.

◈ **Unicorn:** The unicorn is a slender, white horse with a spiraling horn on its forehead. The horn represents the development of one's intuition through visualization, with the spiraling horn symbolizing the third eye. The unicorn is the most magical of mystical creatures, and it is a good omen if you are lucky enough to encounter one. Legend says the blood of the unicorn has healing properties, making it most valuable to anyone in need of healing. Dust filed from the horn is used as protection against poisons and diseases. In Medieval tapestries, the unicorn was used as a symbol to represent Christ.

◈ **Valkyries** are minor female deities, who serve Odin, the chief of Gods in Norse mythology. Their purpose is to choose the most heroic of those who have died in battle and to carry them off to Valhalla (Odin's hall) where they became einherjar (spirits of warriors who had died bravely in battle). Odin needed warriors to fight by his side at the pre-ordained battle of the end of the world. A wolf is the valkyrie's mount, but the appearance of the valkyrie herself is raven-like. She flies over the battlefields choosing corpses for Odin's army. Therefore, the wolves and ravens that scavenged the aftermath of battles serve a much higher purpose, then just ordinary scavengers. The Celtic legend of the Morrigan has similar characteristics.

◈ **Vampires** subsist on human and/or animal life force by draining the human or animal of its blood. Ways to destroy the vampire: driving a wooden stake through its heart, decapitation, or incinerating the body completely, and scattering the ashes. Some objects used to ward off vampires are garlic, sunlight, a branch of wild rose, the hawthorn plant, holy water, a crucifix, or a rosary. Vampires cast no shadow nor have a reflection, perhaps due to having no soul. They may not enter one's home/apartment unless invited in, but once they have that invitation they may come and go as they please without further permission.

◆ **Wendigos** are malevolent, cannibalistic, supernatural beings having great spiritual power from Native American mythology. They are strongly associated with the direction North or Winter, coldness, famine, and starvation. Wendigos are also associated with gluttony, greed, and excessiveness, as they are never satisfied after killing and consuming one person because they are constantly on the lookout for new victims. Humans who become greedy and are never satisfied with what they have will turn into a Wendigo. Thus, the myth served as a method of encouraging cooperation and moderation. Maybe this myth needs to be used more in modern times to curb our appetites for always wanting more.

◆ **Werecats** are shape-shifters, who are similar to werewolves, but who take on the feline form (a domestic house cat, lion, panther, etc.). However, they are not influenced by lunar cycles; they can shape-shift when necessary.

◆ **Werewolf** or lycanthrope is a person who shape-shifts into a wolf or wolf-like creature, either purposely, by using magic, or after being placed under a curse with the transformation taking place during the three days of the full moon. They may be killed, if shot with a silver bullet, and have an aversion to the herb wolfsbane. Unlike vampires, religious artifacts such as a crucifix or holy water do not harm werewolves. The werewolf is cunning, merciless, and kills and eats humans without hesitation. Lycanthropy either is a hereditary condition or transmitted by the bite of another werewolf. They disdain vampires, and vice versa.

◆ **Will-o'-wisps** are mischievous spirits of the dead or other supernatural beings attempting to lead humans, who are out at night, astray. It is said that a will-o'-wisp marks the spot of buried treasure in the ground, and that the only time the treasure is retrievable is on Midsummer's Eve (June 20 or June 21). If a person became lost in the woods, and depending on how the spirit is treated, the will-o'-wisp will either cause the person to become more lost or guide them out. The term will-o'-wisp is also used to refer to the ghostly lights sometimes seen at night or at twilight that hover over damp ground (marshes, bogs, wetlands) or along roadsides and railroads. It looks like a flickering ball of light, which recedes if approached.

◈ **Witte Wieven** are spirits of wise women in Dutch legends. They are wise women, herbalists, and medicine healers of the villages or towns. They were also sought for their prophecy and ability to look into the future. As their communities hold them in high esteem at the time of their deaths, ceremonies are held at their gravesites to honor them. Their spirits are thought to remain on earth after they had passed on, which either helped or hindered people they encountered, and they reside in cemeteries or other sacred places. It is thought that the mist in the cemeteries and other sacred places are the spirits of these wise women, which people would bring them offerings and ask for help.

◈ **Wraith** is a being of power that does the bidding of a greater spirit. They have no other purpose for existing other than that of their master(s). They feed on humans' emotions and strengths because without these they would cease to exist. The classic depiction of a wraith is the image of a tall, faceless, humanoid figure shrouded in a black cloak, with long, sharp fingers.

◈ **Zombie** is a re-animated or undead human body devoid of a soul. Stories of zombies originated in the Afro-Caribbean spiritual belief system of Voodoo. A dead person can be revived by a bokor/Voodoo sorcerer, and remain under the control of that bokor, as the zombie has no will of its own. A more ghoulish version of zombies has come from modern horror fiction books and movies. These zombies are brought back from the dead by supernatural or scientific means, and they are known to eat the flesh (or the cerebral matter) of the living.

NAMASTE
(Pronounced "nah-mah-STAY")

Namaste is a combination of the two Sanskrit words: *nama*, and *te*. Basically, *nama* means "to bow" and *te* means "you" Namaste is a greeting for all ages, all genders, and all races. The namaste salutation was transmitted from ancient India to the countries of Southeast Asia, and has now traveled virtually all over the globe. Namaste is recognition that we are all on equal standings, all of us are children of the Divine—we are all one. Namaste is may also be used as a closing notation in written communications similar to sincerely, best regards, love.

The God/Goddess within me acknowledges the God/Goddess within you; is one translation for namaste.

NETI POT

A neti pot is a small ceramic pitcher (similar to a very small teapot). It is filled with warm salt water to cleanse your nasal passages. Hopefully, this sinus wash will become part of your weekly or monthly routine. This cleansing routine will relieve symptoms associated with colds, flu, sinus infections, nasal dryness, allergies, and other sinus irritations, and helps reduce swelling of the nasal membranes.

Neti Pot Instructions:

✳ Fill the neti pot with lukewarm water. Add 1/8 teaspoon of sea salt to the water, and stir to dissolve. Do not use salt with iodine added.

✳ Lean your head to the right and sideways, chin slightly pointing upwards. This may be done over the sink or you may want to do this while in the shower or bathtub. It may take you a few tries to get a comfortable position.

* Gently place the spout of the neti pot flushed or inside your right nostril, forming a seal to avoid any outer leakage, if possible.

* Open your mouth slightly. Breathe continuously through your open mouth during this cleansing procedure. This allows a necessary air passageway so that the water will not drain from behind your nose into your mouth. You'll know if you are doing it wrong.

* Tip the neti pot, allowing the water solution to pour into your right nostril. Within a few seconds, the water will naturally drain from your left nostril into the sink, shower, or bathtub.

* Remove the spout from your right nostril, and exhale through both nostrils. Gently blow your nose into a tissue, or your hand, if in the shower/bathtub.

* Repeat for the other side.

* Thoroughly clean your neti pot after each use. Periodically place it in your dishwasher for thorough sanitizing. Everyone in the household should have their own neti pot.

* You may notice improved breathing, smelling, and tasting. As with anything, the more you use the neti pot, the more comfortable you become with it. If you experience any discomfort, please discontinue using your neti pot and consult your doctor or other health care provider.

Ogham

The ancient Celts never wrote anything down, but the Druids[10] did use an alphabetical code that they carved into standing stones or wooden wands. Named after Oghma, the Irish God of Eloquence, the script is known as Ogham, pronounced "o'ham." Each line or series of lines represents a letter of the alphabet, they are also linked with the names of trees. *Example:* A—ailm, pine, or white fir. Ogham inscriptions are believed to have been one of the chief tools of communication between the Druids, acting as a storehouse of encoded knowledge.

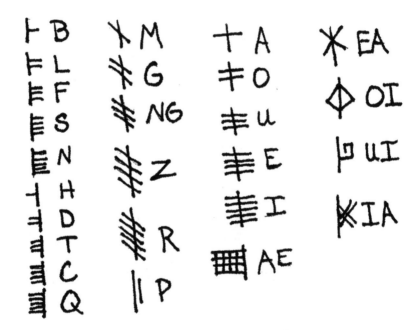

---

10 Druids are ancient Celtic shamans. The male druids wore white robes/capes; the female druids wore black robes/capes.

PENDULUM

Pendulums or Dowsing Rods may be used to answers questions, find lost objects, find water, map dowsing, etc. A pendulum may be made from anything, crystals, stones, pieces of metal, glass, etc. You can find them in metaphysical or natural health stores and, of course, over the internet. You may also use your dangling earrings that you wear every day. If your earring is the hook kind, you can just dangle it from a paper clip. Hold the paper clip so that the earring is able to swing freely, and ask your question(s).

If a pendulum catches your eye, feels right, speaks to you, this is the one that you are meant to have, so purchase it. You may make your own with some wire, string, or chain by attaching a crystal, gemstone, bead, etc. to one end. Anything may be used as a pendulum as long as it is able to swing freely. The more that you work with your favorite pendulum, the more responsive it becomes to your energy.

You will need to cleanse your pendulum of the negative energy that is attached to it before using it. You may hold it under running water to cleanse it of negative energy. You may set it out in the moonlight (preferably the full moon) all night, if possible, but if you are not able to place it outside in the moonlight, a windowsill will do. You may also cleanse the pendulum by placing it in a glass bowl/cup filled with sea salt and leave it for two to five hours, or more if necessary.

When you first purchase or make your pendulum, you may want to carry it on your person, either in your pocket, your bra, hold it, or just have it near you for the first 24 hours of acquiring it, so that it becomes use to your energy. At night, I place mine by my bed, and have sometimes placed it under my pillow.

Pendulums swing in vertical straight lines, horizontal straight lines, and in circular movements. You may assign each directional swing a "response" by first asking the pendulum to show you what a certain response looks like. E.g., "What does "no" look like?" or "What does "yes" look like?" or "What does "maybe" or "neutral" look like?" Your pendulum may swing vertical for "yes." However, you also may tell your pendulum that horizontal is "yes," and vertical is "no," just do what feels right for you. You may want to test your pendulum's response the first few times that you use it by asking questions that you know the answer to. This is done so that your pendulum and you become familiar with each other.

You do not have to swing your pendulum it will swing on its own. Some people think they have to wake up the pendulum by starting the swing. It will swing when you ask it a question. Sometimes it many take a few seconds to start swinging, but it will swing. Let go of your old belief patterns, fears, and doubts, before using your pendulum, and it will swing more freely because you are not sub-consciously holding it back.

There are ABC charts that you may get from books or from the internet to use with your pendulum. When using the ABC charts, your pendulum will spell out the response, which gives you a chance to ask questions that do not require a "yes" or "no" response. In the beginning, this is somewhat slow as it spells out the words, but the more you use this method, the more you and your pendulum become attuned to the chart(s).

*Example*s: Below are a couple of questions that may be answered with a positive, negative, maybe, or neutral response.

1) Will I get the job that I applied for? *good example*
2) Will I have a boy or girl? *bad example*
3) Will I meet someone at the concert tonight?
   maybe or neutral example, because you will meet people tonight
4) Will I meet a new love interest at the concert tonight?
   good example

Make sure that you tell your pendulum to stop after each question is answered. If you do not, the swinging motion and energy from the previous question is still active. By asking or telling your pendulum to stop, you break the connection of the previous question to the present question. Just simply say, "stop," and it will stop moving.

A few pendulum tips:

* To keep track of your pendulum sessions: keep a journal/notebook available to write down your questions and record your pendulum's responses.

* Use your instincts to reassure yourself that the responses you receive are correct. Over time, this will become easier to ascertain; especially, the more you surround yourself with your angels, spirit guides, God/Spirit, when you work with your pendulum. This only allows positive energy in.

* If you have different pendulums, they may have different swings (e.g., big swinging motion or barely moving). You may establish your own directional swings when programming your pendulum by telling it the "yes" response, etc.

* Clear your pendulum as often as possible, and if possible, after each use. This will ensure that positive energy is able to work with your pendulum; there is nothing blocking the positive energy from coming in.

Prep before using your pendulum:

* When you use your pendulum to do a reading, clear your space by standing in the center of the room/area and ask that all negative energy be changed to positive. Your pendulum will swing in a circle, or back and forth. Ask that Spirit or your angels stop your pendulum when it is finished. This may take two or three minutes, if the area needs clearing. You may even feel a difference in the energy of the room. While clearing your area, your pendulum may go in one direction, then change and go the other way. Do not judge the swing of the pendulum; just let it go until it is finished.

* You may also want to do this: pendulum your palm and ask that you become balanced and charged with positive energy. Do not question the direction the pendulum

swings; just let Spirit or your angels do the work. This may take a few seconds. Your pendulum will stop when the balancing/clearing work is complete.

* Then you can pendulum your chart(s)/tools; ask that they be surrounded by Love, Light, positive energy, and the absolute truth.

* Invite your angels, spirit guides, God (Spirit/Source/Universe), your ancestors, fairies, and ascended masters, etc. in to surround you with Love, Light, positive energy, and the absolute truth.

* You can say something such as this: "I am an open, clear, perfect, and pure channel connected to God. I am communicating with God only and no one else, except those who are assigned to me and all of this is for my highest and greatest good. The messages I receive are the absolute truth because I am safe, loved, and protected by God, and all of this is done in Love and Light and for the greater good of all concerned." Then begin.

* After a while, you may not have to go through all of this each time you use your pendulum. Especially after your pendulum gets use to your energy and you have worked in a certain room/area for a while and have cleared it many times of negative energy.

PENTAGRAM

The pentagram (a five-pointed star) has magical meanings with people who practice Neo-Pagan faiths, which they incorporate into jewelry, clothing, etc. Early Christians used the pentagram to represent the five wounds of Christ (palms, feet, and abdomen). The symbol is also associated with the Freemasons (Masons), and the Order of the Eastern Star (female segment of the Masons). This symbol was used by the early Christians to represent the five senses: sight, hearing, taste, smell, and touch. In modern times, it is used represent: Earth, Air, Fire, Water, and Spirit.

It has also been associated with the planet Venus. Every eight years, Venus' orbit around the zodiac is in the design of a pentagram. The Pentagram was connected to the worship of the Goddess Venus, the Morning Star (Eastern Star), the source of light and knowledge. The word "pentacle" is sometimes used as an alternative name for pentagram.

Due to misunderstanding of symbols used in ceremonial magic, this symbol became associated with Satanism and eventually rejected by Christians sometime in the 20th Century. With the single point, pointing upwards it depicts the spirit presiding over the four elements of matter, and is good. The topmost point, points towards heaven, which is the seat of wisdom. With the point reversed, it is perversion and evil because it overturns the proper order of things and demonstrates the triumph of matter over spirit (the goat of lust attacking the heavens).

The pentagram has come to represent the four elements with the addition of Spirit. Earth, the upper point, Air, upper right point, Fire, lower right point, Water, lower left point, Spirit, upper left point. An outer circle around the pentagram is seen as binding the elements together or bringing them into harmony; with the added circle, it is referred to as a "pentacle." Some people think that by displaying this symbol in jewelry, clothing, home, office, etc. it is a show of support for demonic practices. You could say that people who think this way are very narrow-minded, misinformed, misguided, ignorant, so on and so on.

It is the state symbol for the State of Texas. It is the shape of the Pentagon building in Washington, DC, and the city itself is laid out in the shape of a pentagram. This is one very important symbol, but with different meanings to different groups and sects. So, this shape isn't bad or evil, is it?

 Pentagram

PLANTS AND FLOWERS

The use of plants and flowers is a way to bring in prosperity, abundance, harmony, etc. into one's home, living area, or workspace. Feng Shui is the ancient Chinese practice of the arrangement and placement of objects in space, or space around objects, to achieve harmony with the environment. It is used to affect the health, wealth, and personal relationships of the people functioning within that space.

❋ Most tropical plants brought indoors will help remove toxins from the air.

❋ Pointed leaves are Yang and move Chi quickly through the room or area. They are best used in a stagnant corner to keep the energy flowing. Prickly plants and those with star-shaped leaves encourage movement.

❋ Fire energy plants or flowers (those red in color) are best in the Fame sector, or the upper-middle section of the room.

❋ Round, floppy leaves are more Yin and tend to be calming in nature.

❋ Bushy plants slow down the Chi as it mingles amongst the leaves. These plants are great for hallways.

❋ Tall plants represent tree energy and need to go in the middle but slightly to the left of the room, or Family sector of the home or office and individual rooms. As tree roots displace the earth, you will need to avoid large, tall, woody plants in the middle of rooms, so as not to interfere with the energy flow.

❋ Fragrant flowers are great for energizing a room, as their aroma moves the energy throughout the area.

❋ Plants in multiples of three may neutralize disharmony in relationships, except in the bedroom (i.e., two's a couple, three's a crowd).

* Use sprawling/ivy type plants to soften sharp edges and corners, but if depression is an issue, use non-plant items like crystals, mobiles, mirrors, etc. If depression is not an issue, by using these plants, which represent Water, they will enhance an entry, especially if the entrance is in the middle of the building.

* Decorating a plant with a string of lights increases its energy.

* Use plants in the kitchen, especially tall tree-like plants which will support the Fire of cooking. A plant between the sink and refrigerator and the stove keeps Water from putting out the Fire.

Properties of specific plants and flowers:

* **Azalea:** helps absorb foam insulation emissions.

* **Apple:** the fragrance of spiced apples lowers blood pressure.

* **Basil:** use the fragrance to uplift spirits & reduce migraines.

* **Bamboo:** uplifting whether living plants or as sticks, flutes, and wind chimes. Use under slanting ceilings and on overhead beams. Associated with longevity and maintaining prosperity. Bamboo absorbs gasses from new furniture and carpet, especially formaldehyde. It also brings in good luck and prosperity.

* **Bonsai:** represents stunted growth and is least harmful in the North.

* **Cactus:** rarely belongs inside, used for protection and helps one's reputation. Planting a cactus outside the window of your child's bedroom discourages negative forces from getting in and discourages the teenager from sneaking out at night.

❀ **Cornflowers:** brings balance to love, family, and work.

❀ **Cut Flowers:** Yang, better in the bedroom than plants.

❀ **Chrysanthemum:** for ease, happiness, and joy; also, helps with absorbing benzene from plastics.

❀ **Daffodil:** attracts wealth and helps with communication and politeness.

❀ **Dandelion:** protects from health problems and other mishaps.

❀ **Day Lily:** flirtatious energy, but too many can undermine health.

❀ **Dieffenbachia:** absorbs toxic emissions from plywood.

❀ **Eucalyptus:** clears sinuses and reduces feelings of being overwhelmed.

❀ **Fern:** Yin, softens the hardest of office furniture, machinery, and electrical equipment. Ferns are a favorite in the Feng Shui gardens. It also soothes insecurities.

❀ **Forget-Me-Not:** use around gravesites and sparingly in home garden to remember loved ones.

❀ **Geranium:** lifts the spirits—white flowers promote peace of mind; red flowers bring prosperity when placed on both sides of the front and back doors.

❀ **Gourd(s):** placed outside the front door of your dwelling, room, or workspace will dispel negative energy from entering. Gourds are also used to travel between the two realms—spiritual and physical.

❀ **Holly:** attracts an abundant income.

❀ **Hollyhock:** promotes fertility.

* **Ivy:** softens edges of furniture and protruding corners.

* **Jade (money plant/friendship tree):** brings prosperity.

* **Juniper:** promotes longevity in relationships.

* **Lemon, Lime, or Orange Trees:** these trees counteract exhaustion, and they are good for prosperity.

* **Lilacs:** purple and blue flowers are more favorable for creativity; white flowers are considered somewhat disruptive.

* **Lotus:** a most spiritual plant; enhances creativity and sensuality.

* **Marigolds:** for cheering, but too many may contribute to depression.

* **Mint:** eases mental fatigue.

* **Magnolia:** truth and honesty.

* **Peace Lily:** balances radiation from TV/computers; absorbs toxins from detergents.

* **Peony:** attracts love, and brings honor and wealth.

* **Philodendron:** prosperity.

* **Pine:** symbol of longevity—whether in life or relationships.

* **Plum Tree:** very positive, promotes longevity.

* **Rose:** associated with beauty; white—clarity; red—protective; yellow—intellectual pursuits; and pink—attracts love.

* **Snake Plant:** absorbs formaldehyde from the air.

* **Spider Plant:** depressing, but great at absorbing toxins.

* **Tulips:** the epitome of love: red sets the heart on fire, as well as devotion; yellow and variegated inspires one to fight for loved ones.

* **Yew:** very protective.

Tips—plants and flowers:

* If you want children, you should avoid placing flowers in the bedroom. Your bedroom is an area to generate energy for resting and romance. By placing a basket of fruit (any fruit will do) for their soft gentle energy, as they are the "children of nature," they represent the fertility of nature. Pomegranates are a symbol of fertility—they represent the ovaries filled with eggs.

* Place a bowl of oranges, limes, or lemons at the main entrance of the house or dwelling to ward off evil spirits or negative influences from entering.

* Fill your office with soft plants to generate more energy. Houseplants promote business growth and brighten any workspace. Place plants in the east, south, or southeast corners of your office to attract good luck.

* Clean out the clutter in your home/dwelling (even your office/workspace). The presence of this clutter represents choked energy; the positive energy is being prevented from flowing freely throughout your home, office, etc. It prevents or stifles the flow of love, wealth, prosperity, and health to and in your home, dwelling, etc. The energy becomes stuck; it is not allowed to keep moving freely, by keeping the Chi alive, well, and happy.

* The three regions in your home that strongly affect your love life are the space around your front door; the relationship area; and the bedroom. Make these as inviting and clutter free as possible, otherwise the love

energy becomes stagnant and eventually dies because it is not able to move around, move forward, or continue to grow.

❋ The main door to a dwelling or room is the "Mouth of Chi," as it strongly influences the flow of Chi into your house, dwelling, or workspace. Keep this area as clutter free as possible, so that you encourage the good Chi.

❋ Wind chimes are an inexpensive Feng Shui tool that are easy to place anywhere in the home, office, room, etc. to enhance Chi or good energy. They are used to dissolve Shar Chi (bad energy) with the tones of their energy. Wind chimes are not only aesthetic and pleasing to the ear, but they are useful in modifying dwellings or large structures due to bad Feng Shui.

PSYCHOMETRY

Psychometry is a form of divination or ESP in which information is intuited from an object. Psychic vibrations are communicated to the psychic reader when the object is touched. Mental imagery or feelings will emerge about the people who handled the object. Sometimes, in attempts to solve cases of missing persons, psychometry is used. Gypsy fortunetellers used their gift of psychometry by asking for a piece of silver as payment for a palm or card reading. While giving the palm or card readings, the Gypsy receives information from the coin that was previously handled by the client. Also, psychometry is used to learn historical significance about a particular object.

REIKI ENERGY HEALING
(Pronounced "ray-key")

Reiki is a Japanese technique for stress reduction and relaxation that also promotes healing. It is administered by "laying-on-hands" and is based on the idea that an unseen "life-force energy" (Chi/Qi/Prana) flows through us and is what causes us to be alive. If your life-force energy is low, then you are more likely to become sick or feel stressed, and if it is high, you are more capable of being happy and healthy.

A treatment feels like a wonderful, glowing radiance, that flows through and around you—a "spiritual massage." Reiki treats the whole person—body, emotions, mind, and spirit. It creates many beneficial effects that include relaxation and feelings of peace, security, and well-being. Many people who have received Reiki treatments have reported miraculous results.

Reiki is a simple, natural, and safe method of spiritual healing and self-improvement that everyone can use. It is effective in helping virtually every known illness and malady and always creates a beneficial effect. It also works in conjunction with other medical or therapeutic techniques to relieve side effects and promote faster recovery.

The word Reiki is made-up of two Japanese words—Rei, which means "God's Wisdom" or "the Higher Power;" and Chi, which is "life-force energy." Reiki may be referred to as "spiritually guided life-force energy."

While Reiki is spiritual in nature, it is not a religion (it has no dogma). Reiki does not depend on belief at all and will work whether you believe in it or not.

A Reiki practitioner directs the Universal energy or power into the client's body, which unblocks their Chi—their own personal energy. The Reiki energy helps their Chi move freely and in turn promotes balance in their body and life, which leads to a healthier existence.

A Reiki practitioner is one who is attuned to the energy of Reiki via a Reiki Master. To become a Reiki practitioner, you will need to go through several levels of attunements—Level 1, Level 2, and Level 3—the Master Level.

The best way to keep your Chi moving freely and to stay positive is by making an effort each day to focus on the good in your life, the world, and the universe. This will keep the negative thoughts and negative energies from entering your psyche and draining your life-force energy, your Chi. The only way to do this is to make it a priority to focus on the positive; otherwise, this will never happen.

Most Reiki practitioners charge a fee from $45 to $65 for an hour session and $90 to $120 for an hour-and-half session. Reiki gets the gunk out of your system so that your body is able to do its job by keeping you healthy and happy. To learn more about Reiki, go to your natural or alternative health store. The natural health stores should have the services offered there or have a list of Reiki practitioners.

Reiki Power Symbol:  Cho Ku Rei

RINGS AND FINGERS

The Symbolism of Rings:

Rings are a symbol of unity and eternity. At one time, a ring's circular shape was associated with the sun and moon, therefore, making them magical and sacred. This gave protection to the wearer by connecting the wearer to the Sun's and Moon's power and energy.

To this day, some of this magical or sacred association influences how and why rings are worn. The strongest magical tradition that still holds true today is the one surrounding the ring finger, or third finger. This finger was thought to contain a nerve that went directly to the heart. Therefore, by wearing a wedding/engagement ring on this finger, it symbolized the binding commitment and union of hearts. In addition, the ring wearer may not even be aware that they are intuitively placing a ring on a particular finger to invoke that power or meaning of that finger.

The Meaning of Fingers When Wearing Rings:

Right Hand vs. Left Hand: A person's right and left hand represent the conscious and sub-conscious minds. The left hand (sub-conscious) reflects the buried instincts, beliefs, and attitudes of a person. The right hand (conscious) reflects logic and awareness. Wearing a ring on a particular finger may symbolize a person's unknowing wish to strengthen the powers associated with that particular finger, which may reflect a desire to control one's life and actions. If the particular rings you were are set with gemstones, you are including the power or influence of the stone into the finger as well.

Thumb—Self-Control: As the thumb is set apart from the rest of the fingers, and still able to work with them and provide strength at the same time, this is a symbol of self-control or determination. The thumb is a symbol of your outward appearance to the world, what you think of yourself. You use your thumbs to control or direct your actions; without your thumbs, you would have difficulty holding onto items or picking items up. By wearing rings on your thumbs, you are demonstrating your freedom and independence to the world, showing that you are in control.

Index Finger—Power, Goals, or Desires: This finger is referred to as "the pointer," you use it to point out what you desire, what you wish to exert power over. You are told it is rude to point your finger at others, and this is why: You are directing your authority over others, as it is usually done in anger or in ridicule. In years past, kings, priests, and healers wore rings on the index fingers for this reason, the power and goal the pointer indicated. Because of this association, medicines were applied to the body with the index finger, which was thought or said to give speed and power to the medicines' effects.

Middle Finger—Individuality, Generosity, or Greed: The middle finger, the longest finger on the hand, gives the impression of one's role in life. It shows your individuality, that you are different by wearing a ring on this finger. It is also used in a vulgar display of anger, flipping someone the bird/giving them the finger. Those who wear rings on their middle fingers are seen as well balanced. However, it may also be an unconscious indication that they want to be or enjoying being the center of attention.

Ring Finger—Passion, Feelings, and Creativity:
It was once believed that the third finger had a direct connection to the heart, the place where our soul are kept. Because of this belief, the third finger is said to represent our passions, feelings, and creativities. By wearing a wedding or engagement ring on this finger—the ring finger, and the implication of its association with the heart, this proclaimed your commitment to your love interest. However, if the ring has nothing to do with a love interest, this symbol shows you are committed to yourself, your ideas, feelings, artistic creativities, etc.

Little Finger—Relationships: The little finger
demonstrates your attitude towards other people, sex, and the material world. Rings worn on your little finger is a show of confidence and independence in relationships, no matter if the relationships are personal or business. Rings on the little finger, the pinky, show that you know what you want and you go for it. By wearing "pinky rings," it is also an expression of your sex appeal and your attitude towards sexuality.

Nose Rings: Originally worn for the belief that
they stop the entry of spirits into the body.

Earrings: Earrings were once believed to hinder
the entry of evil spirits. If the earrings have gemstones in them, the qualities or healing powers of the stones become connected to the psyche; the simple way to improve your body, mind, and spirit.

Toe Rings: Toe rings in Western culture are worn
as a fashion statement and usually only on the second toe of the foot—the longest one. Toe rings are also worn as a marital status in the Hindu culture. The toe ring worn in this fashion is called bichiya (pronounced *"bee-chee-ya"*).

Cleansing Your Jewelry:

Your jewelry should be cleansed of negative energy before it is worn. Refer to *Cleansing Your Crystals/Stones* section of this book for how to cleanse your jewelry. To charge a piece of jewelry, you may leave it in the light of the full moon, outside in direct moonlight, or inside on a windowsill. Wearing the piece of jewelry puts an energy imprint on it. Day to day events such as your emotions (especially negative ones), dirt, natural body oil, etc. build up over time, so you may want to cleanse and empower your jewelry as often as you can.

Jewelry tips:

Wearing the same amount of jewelry on each side of your body is very balancing. Wearing more on one side then the other, throws your body off balance. *Example:* Two bracelets on the left arm, needs to be balanced with say, two bracelets on the right arm, or two rings on the right hand. Or maybe, one necklace with one ankle bracelet, or two earrings in one ear, with two earrings in the other ear, and maybe one bracelet on the left wrist with one ankle bracelet on the right ankle, etc. Be creative, this is just fun to do, and by adoring yourself with jewelry, colorful or fine clothing, makeup, etc. is a way to honor the Goddess/God in you.

RUNES

Rune Casting is not fortunetelling in the sense that you see the future; runes like tarot, are oracles from which one seeks advice. The rune caster (the one casting the runes: you) will use their intuition to decipher the cast. The ability to read runes is an acquired skill that does develop over time. As with anything of this nature, the more you practice, the more you trust your intuition, and the more conformable you become using your runes.

Most sets have 33 runes. I use a set of 12 runes I found in a book by Scott Cunningham, *Living Wicca*. You may create your own 12-piece set via Scott Cunningham's book or there is an example rune sheet at the end of this rune section. You will need flat smooth stones (unpolished is best) of the same size to mark the rune figure on. I purchase my small flat unpolished stones from a local nursery, and use paint or a fine point Sharpie (color of your choice) to write the rune figure onto the stone.

Runes may be used to help you analyze the path that you are on and the possible outcome. Remember, the future is not fixed; it changes with everything you do. So, if you do not like the prediction from the rune casting, you have the power to change your path/future. The runes may be used to point out the possibility of your future, to show you where you are headed.

The word "rune" means mystery, secret, or whisper. Each rune character has an obscure or difficult to understand meaning and property associated with it. In ancient times, runes were used for writing, divination, and magic, which represented the forces of nature and mind. In addition, each rune has a relationship, or a story, that the Norse associated with their Gods (e.g., Thor, Odin, Freya). The rune alphabet is made by using straight lines for the ease of cutting into stone or wood. Even though some modern books and rune sets have a blank one, there cannot be a blank rune, because a rune is a symbol, or a letter of an alphabet.

Finally, just practice with your runes, get to know them, have fun with them, so that you become comfortable in casting. Cast for yourself, your family, and friends to become familiar with the readings/interpretations and to learn to trust your intuition.

There are many books for further study, and info is readily available via the internet. One website I used is http://sunnyway.com/runes/, but there are many. This particular website has a page called "Write in Runes," where you enter your name to have it spelled using the rune alphabet, very cool.

How to Rune Cast

You want to be in a quiet place, if possible. Place a small cloth on the surface in front of you, because you will be working with the runes on this cloth. This cloth is used to protect your runes from getting dirty and forms a boundary for the casting. However, it is not <u>necessary</u> to have this cloth. Also, keep your runes in a bag or box to keep them contained in one area. For some of the castings you will need to pull them one at a time from the bag or box.

Scattering/Freefall:

◎ Clear your mind and carefully form a question. Take your time. Concentrate on your question, and only that question. Changing your mind/question only confuses the situation. I usually ask, "What is in store for me?" This is very generic, but most of the time I either have way too much clutter/chatter running around in my mind, which makes it difficult to concentrate. Once you have the question in your mind, begin to mix the runes in the bag/container/your hands. Continue to do this for a few seconds.

◎ Runes are oracles, and oracles are often obscure. Each rune has many different meanings and it is up to the rune caster to interpret how the meanings apply to the question at hand. You may get even deeper interpretations through your own "gut" reactions to the rune's definition.

◎ Scatter the runes onto your cloth, by dropping them, all at once. Read the runes that land face up. These will relate to the current situation and the circumstances that led to it. How the runes are read is largely subjective, but in general, runes lying in the center are the most immediately relevant, while those lying around the edges are less important, or represent influences that are more general.

◎ Another way to read is starting at the top of the cast circle, going clockwise (right to left).

◎ Runes that are close together or touching often complement each other, or may represent a single thing, while runes that fall on opposite sides of the pattern frequently represent opposing influences. Some runes will land off the cloth area, these you can disregard or ignore for this reading.

◎ Rune readings are based on the rune caster's opinions or feelings (intuition). Look at the patterns and relationships that appear in each reading and see what interpretations make sense to you.

Five-Rune Layout:

◎ Select five runes from the bag or box that you keep them in, one at a time, without looking at them, and lay them face down on the rune cloth. (This is why it is important that your runes be as close to the same size/shape as possible, so that you cannot identify them by their shape.) Three runes are placed horizontally side by side, representing past, present, and future. Another rune is placed above the center and the final one is placed below the center. Turn all the runes face-up.

◎ Read the center rune first. This one represents today/present, and will show your problem or issue as it is now. It can also show your state of mind. A negative rune in this position, that does not seem to be in synch with the question, can often show that you may be in a distressed/agitated state of mind. If this is the case, it may be best if you do the rune casting after you have calmed your mind (i.e., do not do this when you are angry).

◎ The rune to the left of the center rune, signifies the past and will tell you what it was in the past that caused you to be in your current position. This past could be the immediate past (i.e., yesterday, last week, last month, etc.), not necessarily years ago.

- ◎ Next, read the rune lying above the center. This indicates how you may reach the outcome and may show you the help that you can expect to receive in reaching this. If there is a negative rune here, it may indicate an unwillingness to accept the advice given by the runes or another person, or it may indicate delays or slight problems that may impede the speedy resolution of the matter in question.

- ◎ The rune below the center one indicates what part of the problem must be accepted and cannot be changed or what may hinder you from reaching the outcome. Positive runes here show a lack of troublesome influences and oppositions, while negative runes show the obstacles to your success.

- ◎ The rune to the right of the center one is the final-result rune. This rune indicates the final-outcome, regarding the other issues in the rune cast.

- ◎ This rune cast indicates recent future happenings, usually within three months. Remember, you have the power to change your path/future.

Before you begin the rune cast:

- ◎ Invite your angels, spirit guides, God (Spirit/Source/Universe), your ancestors, fairies, and ascended masters in and ask them to surround you with Love, Light, and positive energy.

- ◎ You can say something such as this: "I confirm that I am an open, clear, perfect, and pure channel connected to God. I am communicating with God only and no one else, except those he assigns to me for my highest and greatest good. And the messages I receive are the absolute truth because I am safe, loved, and protected by God and all of this is done in Love and Light and for the greater good of all concerned." Then begin.

Rune Positions
Example 1

Will help you getting to the outcome

Past   Current/Present   Outcome

May hinder you getting to the outcome
or could be neutral having no affect at all

Rune Positions
Example 2

What is happening   What is going to   What is meant to
now (present)   happen (future)   be (destiny/fate)

List of Runes

Comfort	ease, pleasure, security, joy happiness, a turn for the better	**Death**	the end of a matter, new beginnings, initiation, changes, purification
Disordered thoughts	emotional tension, doubt, irrationality, confusion	**Gifts**	legacies, promotions, windfalls also physical gifts, psychic and spiritual gifts, sacrifices, giving of oneself
The Home	family, relations, foundations stability, self-image	**Love**	emotional states, romance, spouse/partner difficulties or influences
Man	a male influence, a man; protection, a shield	**Poison**	gossip, slander, negativity, baneful habits, harmful attitudes
Possessions	safety/abundance, inherited property, possessions, a home, or bad karma & prejudices; also aids in spiritual and physical journeys	**War**	conflicts, quarrels, anger, hostility, aggression, confrontation
Wealth	money, financial concerns, employment, employers	**Woman**	a female influence, a woman; nurturing, loving, caring

SABBATS AND WHEEL OF THE YEAR

The Wheel of the Year is a term used by Wiccans and Neo-Pagans regarding Mother Earth's seasons. There are eight festivals, spaced evenly throughout the year and referred to as "Sabbats" by the Wiccans. Four of the Sabbats, held during the time of the solstices and equinoxes, are referred to as "quarter days." The other four Sabbats fall approximately midway between the quarter days, are referred to as "cross-quarter days." These eight festivals or holidays honor Mother Earth's seasons. As we celebrate these holidays, we are lending our energies to the turning of the Wheel, and by working with these energies of Nature; we are no longer struggling against the natural cycle of life on Mother Earth.

Sabbats:

❈ **Samhain** (Oct 31): Halloween, Celtic New Year

❈ **Yule** (Dec 21): Winter Solstice

❈ **Imbolc/Bridgid's Day** (Feb 2): Spring begins

❈ **Ostara** (March 21): Spring Equinox

❈ **Beltane** (May 1): May Eve or May Day, Summer begins

❈ **Litha/Midsummer** (June 21): Summer Solstice

❈ **Lammas/Lughnasadh** (Aug 1): Summer ends, Fall begins

❈ **Mabon** (Sept 21): Fall/Autumn Equinox

SANSKRIT

Sanskrit is the prayer language of Hinduism and is described as "the language of the Gods." This language, dating back to 3,500 BC, is thought to be the origin of all Indo-European languages. All ancient Indian philosophy and yogic scriptures were written in Sanskrit. To unleash the countless secrets buried in these ancient texts, knowledge of Sanskrit is imperative. These sounds create energy vibrations that replace negative energy with positive energy.

Websites regarding Sanskrit:
http://www.swargarohan.org/Glossary.htm
http://learn-sanskrit.com/sanwords.htm
http://www.hinduwebsite.com/hinduism/h_meaning.asp

SCRYING

Scrying has been used for centuries as a way of seeing or understanding the past, present, or future and is achieved by using different types of media. The media used are crystals, stones, glass, mirrors, water, fire, or smoke. Whichever media used, it is a way to help the scryer focus their mind and visually see what is going to happen or what has taken place. The visions are thought to come from God/Creator or those assigned to communicate with us (i.e., angels, spirit guides, or one's higher self through the sub-conscious).

SMUDGING

Smudging is used to clear yourself and your area of negative energies. Your area is your home, office, work area, or any area that you call your own. As everything is made of energy, there is a need for it to be restored to loving, positive energy as much as possible or when you think or feel it is necessary to do so. Holding this negative or bad energy in us and around us affects the way that we act, it can weaken our immune system, cause depression, sadness, arguments, etc. Before, if possible, you move into a new place, smudge the whole area to rid the energies that are left over from the previous tenants. Even if the place that you move into has not been lived in before, considering the energies that were stirred up with all the actives of the building process, you will still need to smudge. If you are not in the position to smudge before moving in, right after the move will do. You may want to smudge again after you have unpacked and set things up. This will clear your home once again of the negative, unsettled energies that have been released with all the unpacking. This also applies to your office or work area or any area that you wish to clear. The previous person(s) that occupied your desk area or office has left their energy imprint, be it good or bad, it just needs to be cleared, so that you are not having residual affects from the former occupant. You may also want to smudge items that are in your home or office, like your books, office supplies, telephones, etc. or anything that you may handle.

Smudge Ceremony:

* Remember that no matter the details of your actions, God, Source, your angels, or spirit guides know your intent and will bless your efforts.

* Purchase a smudge stick from your local health or herb store, or over the internet. A smudge stick is a bundle of dried herbs, usually white sage, bound with thread or string. However, other herbs may be used as well. Or, you can make up your own smudge incense by using dried herbs, such as dried white sage, dried rosemary, and dried lavender, and burn them on incense charcoal. (*See* Incense in this book.) You may use a stick of incense, if you do not have access to a smudge stick or dried herbs.

* Start with a prayer, such as, "I invoke the Love and Light of God within; I am a clear and perfect channel. Let Love and Light be my guide."

* The smudge stick is sometimes hard to keep smoldering. First, light it then blow out the flame and blow into the smoldering embers or else it may burn out. If it does burn

out, just re-light and keep going. Once the stick is smoldering, ask the smoke to bless and trap all negative entities and energies.

* First, smudge yourself starting with the bottoms of your feet and working the smoke up and around your body, and around your head and crown chakra. Second, start at the doorway of the room by walking clockwise,[11] or to the right, and directing the smoke completely around every room in your home/bedroom/office space. You may also do the closets, chest of drawers, desk drawers, individual items, etc. Use your hand, or special fan that you have to move the smoke around the area(s) you are smudging.

* When you have completely smudged all the areas, say another prayer, thanking God, your angels, and spirit guides for their help and blessings. Ask that the smoke carry all negative entities and energies out and away from your home/bedroom/office. Then put out your smudge stick to use for another time.

* Open as many windows and doors as possible to allow the smoke to be purged from the interior and fresh air and chi to flow back into your home/room/office. The idea is to let the smoke take unwanted energies/entities out through the open windows and doors.

* You may also use a bell(s) or singing bowl(s) to ring as you smudge the area or areas.

* You may want to re-do the smudge ceremony every six months, or more often if you feel the need. You may want to try to time the smudging to a new moon or the changing of seasons. Remember, God, Source, your angels, or spirit guides understand what you are trying to do, so THERE IS NO WRONG WAY to do it. You may want to include some of your favorite readings, or do this with a loved one, but remember just have fun and enjoy this blessed ritual.

---

11 Clockwise is deosil; widdershins is counter-clockwise or anti-clockwise.

SPELLS: HOW TO GET THEM TO WORK

1. Spells or energy work (requests or prayers) cast by you will not work unless you change the way you think. If you keep dwelling on the bad, the bad will keep happening.

2. If you go into the spell half thinking it might work, then it will not work.

3. If you tell others about the spell or energy work, you mix in their energy with yours, and they may attach negative energy or thoughts to it. Their negative energy weighs down the spell, which causes the spell not to work. It is okay to tell them after the changes have taken place due to your workings (prayers) or your spell.

4. A curse only works because the person you cursed believes that it works. Their believing gives the curse energy to make it happen. The rule is harm no one and this means you as well. So, you wouldn't be placing a curse on anyone, would you? Just think if you do, it comes back to you threefold. This also applies to negative thoughts you have of someone, it usually makes the situation worse. Okay, I'll stop with the unsolicited advice.

5. Once you have done the spell, do not think about it again because you hold it to yourself and you have not given it over to the Universe (God) to handle. A spell is a prayer or a request, so let it go and let it happen. Spells take time so do not fret over them. Some spells that are timed to work with the Moon's energy may take a lunar cycle or twenty-eight days before you notice any changes.

SPELL FOR IMPROVING NEGATIVE THOUGHTS

★ Items and ingredients you will need: glass jar with screw top, honey, sugar, water, wooden Popsicle stick, and a permanent marker, such as a Sharpie.

★ On the Popsicle stick, write the name of the person, your name, or whomever is creating the problem(s) or negative thought(s) or action(s) on one side of the stick. Place the stick in the glass jar. Create a mixture of equal portions of honey, water, and sugar. Pour this into the glass jar, filling it 1/3 full. Shake the jar vigorously once each day while thinking loving, peaceful, and positive thoughts. Ask your angels to surround this request or spell with their Love and Light and the person, or you, as a way to send positive energy and thoughts to the situation.

★ While shaking the jar, you might want to say something like "Loving thoughts are being sent to (name of the person) to release this negativity. All of this is done for the highest and greatest good of all concerned. I ask that this request be surrounded with Love and Light. And so it is."

★ Once there is an improvement or the issue(s) has been resolved, pour the mixture out by returning it to Mother Earth and either bury the Popsicle stick or burn it. You may reuse the glass jar after proper cleansing/clearing.

SPRING EQUINOX
Also Ostara or Eostre

The Spring Equinox is one of the two times during the year that the daytime and nighttime are almost exactly 12 hours long; the other time is the Fall Equinox. It is celebrated on March 20 or March 21 and is also known as the maiden phase of the Triple Goddess—birth/re-birth. In years past, Spring was celebrated for the basic reason that food supplies would soon be restored and warmer weather would be returning after the long cold winter.

The Spring Equinox is a great time to start new projects or choose a new direction that you may have thought about or meditated on during the Winter months—hence spring cleaning, out with the old, in with the new. Eostre or Ostara is the name of an ancient German Lunar Goddess that was honored during this time of the year, and has now been transformed into modern day Easter festivities. Modern day Christians celebrate Christ's rising from the dead (re-birth) after his crucifixion on Good Friday, three days prior to Easter morning.

Eostre's chief symbols were the bunny (both for fertility and because her worshipers saw a hare/bunny on the face of the moon) and the egg (symbolic for creation), which is how they became part of our modern day Easter celebrations (bunnies and eggs). The date for Easter changes each year and is calculated to fall on the first Sunday after the first full moon, following the Spring Equinox.

Also, the ancient Egyptians built the Great Sphinx to align directly with the rising sun on the day of the Spring Equinox (vernal equinox). So, this was and is a very special time of year.

SUMMER SOLSTICE
Also Midsummer's Eve or St. John's Eve

Also, known as Midsummer's Eve or St. John's Eve, occurs at dream-time or nightfall on June 20 or June 21. Summer Solstice is the longest day and shortest night of the year. From this time forward, until the Winter Solstice, the days are getting shorter. The Summer Solstice is also known as the mother phase of the Triple Goddess—full of life phase.

Midsummer's Eve is the evening of herbs. The herbs and flowers gathered this night are considered exceptionally potent. St. John's Wort, burdock, and nettle harvested on Midsummer's Eve are hung on doors, windows, or throughout the home for protection. In the past, livestock were also decorated with garlands made of flowers, foliage, and oak leaves.

As fire was an important part of the Midsummer celebrations, people would gather around bonfires or hearth fires. The fire was traditionally made from two sacred woods—fir and oak. People would feast, dance, and jump the fire for luck and fertility. The livestock/cattle were driven through the embers and smoke to rid them of disease and illness. When the fires had burned down, people would carry ashes back to their homes for protection, health, and luck.

Midsummer's Eve is the time when everything is abundant and flourishing. It is also a time when the fairies or faeries are most playful and favorable. So, to encourage their blessings, be sure to leave an offering of milk or sweets outside for them on this magical night. The moon of Midsummer's Eve is referred to as the "Honey Moon." This is a time when the beehives are full of honey, which is gathered and fermented into mead and consumed during the many marriage ceremonies held during this time of year. It is said that whatever is dreamed on this night will come true. Shakespeare knew of the magic of this time of year, as this is evident in the tale *A Midsummer Night's Dream*.

SUPERSTITIONS

Some of our everyday habits, thoughts, and maybe our common sense came from the superstitions of old. The church and the clergy used superstitions to force, frighten, or heavily encourage the illiterate congregations to believe and to worship the dogma or doctrines of the church by encouraging superstitions.

Animals and Insects Superstitions:

- A frog brings good luck to the house it enters.

- Seeing a single crow is very unlucky; two means good luck; three means health; four means wealth; five means sickness; and six means death.

- If the first butterfly you see of the year is white, you will have good luck all year. Three butterflies together also means good luck.

- Cows lying down, gathered close together next to the fence line, means a rainstorm is coming.

- A wish made upon seeing the first robin in spring will come true, but only if you complete the wish before the robin flies away.

- If a bat gets in your hair, you are possessed by the Devil.

- To dream of a lizard is a sign that you have a secret enemy.

- The Egyptian Goddess Bast was a black, female cat who ruled dancing, music, and pleasure. She bestows good health to all who worship her. Early Christians, wanting to convert people to their faith, convinced the non-believers that black cats were demons in disguise and should be destroyed. Black cats were said to be a witches familiar, which became a belief that people, especially women, who had black cats, as pets were witches. The cats were destroyed, as well, during the witch-hunts or burning times. If a black cat (considered a demon) crossed your path, this would put a barrier of evil between God and you, thus, blocking your entrance to heaven.

- When moving to a new home, always put the cat in through the window instead of the door, so that it will not leave.

- A cricket is a lucky house spirit that takes its luck away when it leaves.

- Dolphins are believed to transport the souls of the dead to the afterlife.

- Butterflies are said to carry messages to the spirit world.

- Carrying a hare's foot is thought to give your good luck, but not good luck for that bunny.

- A ladybug landing on you means very good luck. If the ladybug lands on your hand, this means good weather is coming. The number of spots she has stands for the number of happy months ahead.

- Oysters should only be eaten in months with an "R" in them. Oysters are said to be an aphrodisiac.

- Roosters have long been connected with the sun, they crow to herald its arrival at dawn, and are considered watchful protectors of humans. When a cock crows at midnight, a spirit is passing. If it crows while perched on a gate, or at nightfall, the next day will be rainy.

- You will make a new friend if you run into a spider's web. Finding a spider's web in a doorway means you will have a visitor soon. If you find a spider on your clothes, this means you will be receiving money soon. A spider is thought to be the missing 13th sign of the zodiac based on the 13 lunar months. The spider is associated with psychic abilities, weaving, and women.

Body Superstitions:

- If your ear is burning or ringing, then someone is talking about you. To determine if what is mentioned or thought is good or bad, remember: left for love, right for spite. However, if your right ear itches, someone is speaking well of you; and if your left ear itches, someone is speaking ill of you.

- If your right palm is itchy, money is coming to you, but do not scratch it, as this will stop the money from coming. If your left palm is itchy, then scratch away, as this means that you will soon be paying out money.

- The number of Xs in the palm of your right hand is the number of children you will have.

- If you bite your tongue while eating, it is because you have recently told a lie.

- People with hiccups are thought to be possessed by the Devil.

- People once believed the soul could escape from the body when a person sneezed. To this day, we still say "God Bless You" or "Bless You" when someone sneezes.

- Yawning was thought to be caused by the devil because evil spirits would enter your body when your mouth was wide open. Covering your mouth, while yawning, stops the evil spirits from entering. To yawn was also a sign that danger was near.

- An itchy nose means you are going to have a quarrel with someone. Or, it could mean someone is coming to see you. If it is the right nostril, the visitor will be a male, left nostril, female.

- Cross your fingers for good luck or for making a wish. Bad luck is trapped at the point where the two fingers meet. When you cross your fingers, you stop the bad luck from escaping and interfering with your request, this allows your wish to come true.

- Pulling out a gray or white hair will cause ten more to grow in its place.

- Cutting your hair on Good Friday prevents headaches in the year to come.

- If the right eye twitches, there will soon be a birth in the family. If the left eye twitches, there will soon be a death in the family.

- To cure a sty, stand at a crossroads or intersection and recite "Sty, sty, leave my eye, take the next one coming by."

- If an eyelash falls out, put it on the back of your hand; make a wish, blow on it, and your wish will be granted.

- If the bottom of your right foot itches, you are going to take a trip.

- If you do not cover your baldhead, it will start raining.

- You should not wash your hair the day before an exam. The thought being that you will wash away what you have learned in your prep for the exam.

- Choosing to cut your hair or nails on certain days has particular meanings: Monday for health; Tuesday for wealth; Wednesday for news; Thursday, a new pair of shoes; Friday for sorrow; Saturday, see your true love tomorrow; and Sunday, the devil will be with you all week.

- If you sneeze two or three times in a row, it means that someone is complaining or gossiping about you.

Home Superstitions:

- Never take an old broom with you when moving to a new place as you will bring the negative energies of your previous dwelling to your new one. Always buy a new broom, and it is especially lucky if it is given to you as a housewarming gift.

- Do not lean a broom against a bed because the evil spirits in the broom will cast a spell on the bed (the broom traps negative energy). If you sweep trash out the door after dark, it will bring a stranger to visit. If someone is sweeping the floor and sweeps over your feet, you will never get married. To prevent an unwelcome guest from returning, immediately sweep out the room in which they stayed.

- You sleep best with your head to the north and your feet to the south (this coincides with the Earth's magnetic field). You must get out of bed on the same side that you get in or you will have bad luck. When making the bed, do not stop your task of making it, or you will spend a restless night, and your room looks messy as well.

- Sweeping the area outside your front door each morning will keep the negative energy (or bad spirits) that accumulated during the night swept away by allowing them to enter your dwelling.

- If a front door does not face the street, ill luck will visit the house. You should always close the front door while facing it. It is bad luck to leave a house through a different door than the one used to enter it.

- To cross two forks accidentally is a sign that slander will be spread about you. To drop a fork foretells the visit of a female friend. To stir anything with a fork is to stir up misfortune. And the dropping of a knife foretells the visit of a male friend. Dropping a spoon means that a child or young person will be coming by for a visit or will call you. To cross a spoon over a fork foretells happiness cut short by grief.

- Never pour water into a tumbler that already holds some, for it is an invitation for evil spirits to visit you. You need to drink all the water (or pour out) before you add more. Be Earth friendly, water your plants, and not just pour the water down the drain.

- Spilling wine is a good omen, if done accidentally. However, dropping a glass of wine and breaking the glass, especially by stomping on it, means a happy marriage with enduring lifelong affection.

- Rosemary planted by the doorstep will keep evil spirits away. Ivy growing on a house protects the inhabitants from evil. Mistletoe in the house protects it from thunder and lightning.

- If you leave a rocking chair rocking when empty, it invites evil spirits to come into your house, by inviting them to sit in the rocking chair.

- Mirrors should be covered during a thunderstorm because they attract lightning.

Miscellaneous Superstitions:

- Dropping a pair of scissors is a warning that a lover is unfaithful.

- You must knock on wood three times after mentioning good fortune or the evil spirits will ruin things for you.

- See a penny, pick it up; all day long, you'll have good luck. It is bad luck to pick up a coin if it is tails side up. Good luck only comes if it is heads side up.

- If you give someone an empty purse/wallet, they will never be blessed with riches unless you place a coin or dollar bill inside of it for luck before you give it to them.

- If your shoelace persists in coming untied, take it as an omen that you are about to receive good news.

- When a bell rings, a new angel has received her/his wings.

- To protect yourself from evil, wear a blue bead. The bead is called "an evil eye," which is worn to ward off evil/bad luck.

- If you get a chill up your back or Goosebumps, it means that something bad is about to happen.

- Evil spirits cannot harm you when you stand inside a circle, especially if you sprinkle salt around the circle.

- Clover protects human beings and animals from the spells of those with intent to do harm, and it also protects against the tricks or charms of faeries. It brings good luck to those who keep it in the house.

- To drop a comb/brush while you are combing your hair is a sign of a pending disappointment.

- Step on a crack; break your mother's back (i.e., a crack on a sidewalk or walkway, etc.).

- If two people pull apart the dried breastbone of a chicken or turkey until it cracks and breaks, with each one making a wish while doing so, the person who gets the longer half of the wishbone will have his or her wish come true.

- A watermelon will grow in your stomach if you swallow the seeds.

- A rainbow in the Eastern sky, the morrow will be fine and dry. A rainbow in the Western sky that gleams and glistens, rain tomorrow will fall.

- If you use the same pencil to take a test that you used for studying for the test, the pencil will remember the answers.

- If you catch a falling leaf on the first day of autumn, you will not catch a cold all winter.

- Pick a dandelion that has gone to seed. Take a deep breath and blow the seeds, but make a wish first. If all the seeds blow off, your wish will come true.

- For good luck throughout the year, wear new clothes on Easter.

- Throw back the first fish you catch, then you will be lucky the whole day fishing.

- If you stare into a mirror by candlelight/flashlight, you will see the spirit of a lost loved one.

- When a couple is walking down the street holding hands and an obstacle (such as a lamp post) comes between them, they should say "bread and butter," thereby, keeping the union until the hands meet again on the other side of the lamp post.

- Clinking glasses of alcohol together, as in a toast, is said to scare the spirit(s) out of the alcohol.

- It is bad luck to put up a calendar early or fill in appointments, etc. before the New Year.

- Walking under a ladder is bad luck because the leaning ladder forms a triangle with the wall and ground. Triangles represent the Holy Trinity, and violating the Trinity by breaking it (walking through it) would put you in league with the devil himself. If you must do it, cross your fingers or make the sign of the fig (closed fist, with thumb between index and middle fingers), while walking under the ladder.

- Spilling salt is bad luck for the reason that salt was an expensive commodity, used mainly for medicinal purposes and curing meat/fish. For this reason, spillage was to be avoided at all costs. The idea that it is unlucky to do so may have originated from the belief that Judas spilt salt during the last supper, and as you know, he was doomed. Throwing spilt salt over the left shoulder is linked to its medicinal use. It was thought that evil spirits lurked behind your left shoulder. Throwing salt into their eye (evil eye) was to discourage sickness from invading your body.

- When a halo rings the moon or sun, rain is soon to come. Red skies at night—sailor's delight; red skies at morning—sailor's warning.

- If a dead person's eyes are open, he will find someone to take with him.

- Mirrors in a house of a recently deceased person are covered to prevent the deceased's soul from being trapped in the mirror. All windows are opened at the time of death, so that the soul may leave.

- Seven years of bad luck when breaking a mirror: Mirrors were very expensive in the past and in order to discourage or frighten the servants from breaking the mirrors, they were told that to break them they would receive seven years of bad luck. At the time that this saying came about, the scientists in this time period determined that it took seven years for a human cell to reproduce. So, in order for the curse to be lifted and for things to be new again, it would take seven years.

- Thunder following a funeral means that the dead person's soul has reached heaven.

- The groom should never see the bride the eve of their wedding or their marriage will fail.

- A bride wears a veil to protect her from evil spirits who are jealous or envious of her happy day and union.

- Lucky Bride—something old, something new, something borrowed, something blue, and a lucky sixpence (penny) in her shoe.

- If the groom drops the wedding band during the ceremony, the marriage is doomed.

- The new bride must enter her home by the main door, and must not trip or fall. This is the origin of the custom of carrying the bride over the threshold.

- Marry on the upswing of the clock, the half-hour, like 2:30 instead of 2, or 3. The hands of the clock on their way up, foretell a positive marriage. Hands on their way down, foretell a negative marriage.

- If a child is born with teeth, there is a superstition that it will become extremely selfish.

- For a child to be born with an open hand, however, is a sign of great generosity.

- For the child to cry at the christening is considered a fortunate sign. In the past, it was thought that evil spirits were then leaving the baby's body.

- To predict the sex of a baby: Suspend a wedding band held by a piece of thread over the palm (or stomach) of the pregnant girl. If the ring swings in an oval or circular motion the baby will be a girl. If the ring swings in a straight line the baby will be a boy.

- Ancient Romans thought to put their best foot forward they should always enter a home or building with their right foot. To use their left foot meant they were bringing in unlucky, negative, or evil energy. Right meant good, as in the right hand of God or Gods, and left meant evil, or work of the devil/demons.

- Ancient Celts thought that trees were sacred, and would knock on wood (the tree trunk) to petition the tree spirit for a favor. Later, the Christians used this saying to honor or ask a favor of Christ (the cross was made of wood). So, when they knocked on wood, they were seeking Christ's favor or blessing.

- If you knock your hand accidentally against a piece of wood or a wooden object, it is an indication that you are about to have a love affair. If you knock your hand against iron, however, it is a warning against treachery.

➢ **All Seeing Eye:** Referred to as the "All Seeing Eye" or "Eye of Providence." Used historically as a symbol for the "all knowing." It was quite common in the Renaissance period to use this symbol to represent God, and sometimes enclosed the eye within a triangle to represent the Holy Trinity. The Freemasons eventually adopted this emblem as a symbol for the Great Architect (the Creator). A version of this symbol is on the reverse side of the Great Seal of the United States (first used in 1782), accompanied by the phrase, *Annuit Coeptis*, which means: He has favored our undertakings. The Great Seal, both sides, appear on the back of $1 bill. (Note: the phrase *Novus Ordo Seclorum* also on the reverse side of Great Seal means: New Order of the Ages.)

➢ **Ankh:** Ankh is an ancient Egyptian symbol of life. The horizontal and vertical bars of the lower portion represent feminine and masculine energy, similar to Yin/Yang. The mixture of male/female energy represented with the cross and circle, is a suggestion of fertility and creative power. The top loop, thought to be a symbol of the sun rising on the horizon, is an indication of birth/death/re-birth.

➤ **Bees/Beehives:** Since the beginning of civilization, bees have been very important to humans by providing many of our necessities, such as food, wax for candles, cosmetics, medicines, and pollination of crops and plants. Yes, bees were and are very important to humans. They are the emblem of hard work, industriousness, teamwork, charity, constancy, etc. The image of the bee was used in coats of arms and personal seals, and for any organization that wished to portray any of these characteristics, e.g., the Freemasons. Bees are often regarding as symbols of messages from the heavens.

➤ **Buddha Eyes or Wisdom Eyes:** The small dot between the eyes is a symbol for the third eye, which is the 6th Chakra, the seat of our intuition and imagination, and a symbol of spiritual awakening. The curious squiggle, that looks like a question mark is the Nepali character for number one, which symbolizes the unity of all things as well as the one way to reach enlightenment through the teachings of Buddha.

> **Chakra:** Chakras are vital energy centers in the body that are located along the spine. They are described as balls of energy moving in a spiraling/circular motion. Interruptions to this flow of energy, is believed to cause illnesses, confusion, and emotional difficulties. The movement of energy through the chakras resembles the caduceus symbol and the Kundalini energy.

 Sahasrara: crown chakra, 7th chakra

 Ajna: third eye, 6th chakra

 Visuddha: throat chakra, 5th chakra

 Anahata: heart chakra, 4th chakra

 Manipura: solar plexus, 3rd chakra

 Swadhistana: sacral chakra, 2nd chakra

 Muladhara: root chakra, 1st chakra

➤ **Christogram:** It is a gesture used for the "sign of the cross." The fingers in this position form the Greek letters ICXC, an abbreviation of the Greek name for Christ: IHCOYC XRICTOC, and is used by priests as a gesture in blessings. This hand gesture is seen in Renaissance paintings of Christ, the apostles, saints, and clergy. This same gesture is known in Hindu and Buddhist traditions as the prana mudra, a symbol of healing.

➤ **Caduceus:** It is the wand of the Greek God Hermes (Roman, the God Mercury). This symbol, a winged staff entwined by twin serpents, is nearly universal, found in Egypt, Mesopotamia, and India, where it is always a symbol of harmony and balance. It is used as a symbol to represent the modern day medical field. The caduceus is also a symbol of spiritual awakening, and is linked to the Kundalini energy of Hindu mysticism. Kundalini energy is referred to as a "sleeping serpent" at the base of the spine, the root chakra (1st chakra). However, be very careful in awakening this serpent, it is very powerful energy and is difficult to handle by a novice.

➤ **Cho Ku Rei:** This symbol is the Power symbol in Reiki Energy Healing. Reiki involves the use of Universal Energy to heal. The Reiki practitioner initiates this energy through ancient symbols, which the practitioner is attuned to during their Reiki training. The training consists of three levels of attunements with the third level being the Master level. A Reiki practitioner receives attunements and training from a Reiki Master.

➤ **Cinquefoil or Rose of Venus:** The cinquefoil is a five-leaf rose and is a symbol for the five senses of the human body. It is called the "Rose of Venus," as a reference to the pentagram shape of the orbit of Venus. It was a favorite in coats of arms, and served as a motif for knights who had gained mastery over the self, or self-control. This image eventually became the symbol of silence and secrecy. During the Middle Ages, a rose was suspended from the ceiling of a council chamber, committing those present to secrecy, or "sub Rosa," literally meaning under the Rose.

➤ **Circle:** The circle is the most common and universal sign found in all cultures. It has no beginning or end. It is a symbol of the sun or moon (birth/re-birth), eternity, boundaries, and enclosures. It also represents love in the form of an engagement ring, wedding ring, friendship bracelet, a necklace giving as a gift to a lover, etc.; a circle of love, never ending.

➤ **Compass and Square:** One of the most common symbols of the Masons is the symbol of the compass and square, the architect's tools. This symbol is used to represent the Great Architect of the Universe, the Creator/God. The compass, used to draw circles, which represents Spirit, it also defines and limits beliefs. The square is a symbol for Earth and the material world. When put together—compass and square, they represent the union of matter and spirit, earth and spirit, heaven and earth. The compass and square combined this way forms a hexagram, a six-pointed star also known as the Star of David or Seal of Solomon. *Note:* The "G" that is sometimes displayed in the middle of the compass and square, stands for the Great Architect not God.

➢ **Crescent Moon and Star:** This symbol was originally associated with an ancient Sun God and Moon Goddess. The symbol, adopted by the Ottoman Dynasty,[12] is mainly responsible for its association with Islam. It is used in decorative art, jewelry, national flags, tattoos, etc.

➢ **Eye of Horus:** Horus is an ancient Egyptian Sky God in the form of a raven, and whose mother is Isis and father is Osiris. The eye represents a Peregrine Falcon's eye and the sun, and is associated with Horus' mother, Isis. The mirror image of the eye, the left eye, represents the moon. According to legend, one of Horus' eyes is injured after Osiris was murdered by Set (Horus' uncle). Osiris is the God of the Dead. After Osiris' death, Horus fought Set for the throne of Egypt. In this battle, Horus' eye was injured, which Thoth, the God of Magic, healed. The healing of Horus' eye became a symbol of renewal. The eye became a symbol of healing and protective powers, which is why it is used as a talisman for protection. It also resembles the "All Seeing Eye" or "Eye of Providence" (symbol on the back of the $1 bill).

---

12 This empire ruled from the 15th century to the 20th century in the Middle East countries and settled mostly in what is modern day Turkey.

➢ **Eastern Star:** The emblem of the female sector of the Freemasons is called the "Order of the Eastern Star." The symbol represents the Star of Bethlehem. The planet Venus is also referred to the "Eastern Star." Each point on the star represents a different female biblical hero: Adah, Ruth, Esther, Martha, and Electa, the qualities they stood for, and the representation of the Masonic virtues.

- The book and pillar in the center of the star represent the Masonic sacred law.
- The sword and veil represent Adah, and the virtue of obedience to duty.
- A sheaf of barley represents Ruth, whose virtue is adherence to religious principles.
- The crown and scepter represents Esther, who embodies the virtue of loyalty.
- The broken column represents Martha, and the virtue of endurance in trial.
- The golden cup represents Electa, and the virtue of endurance of persecution.

> **Fleur de Lis:** Also known as the Lily of France. It is said to have originated in the tenth century as a symbol of sovereignty, and was later adopted as the emblem of the French King Louis the VII. However, the symbol is on ancient Greek, Roman, and Celtic coins, making it much older than the tenth century. It is on many coats of arms; and as a Christian symbol linked to the Virgin Mary—lily is a symbol of purity; and is used to represent the Holy Trinity.

> **Goddess:** A familiar symbol used to represent the Goddess, Mother Earth, and/or woman. It is used in jewelry, on pottery, drawings, etc.

➢ **Green Man:** Is a sculpture, stonework, or carving found in churches, garden walls, and on buildings. He is found in many cultures throughout the world and is used as a representation of the vegetation deities. The Green Man is a face surrounded by leaves and vines with branches and vines sprouting from the nose, mouth, nostrils, and other parts of the face. These branches and vines may also have fruits and flowers. Other names for this figure are "Jack in Green" or "Jack of the Green."

➢ **Hamsa:** It is a talisman to protect one against the evil eye. The Jewish name is the Hand of Miriam, in reference to Miriam, the sister of Moses and Aaron. It is a "protecting hand" or "hand of God." An alternative Islamic name is the "Hand of Fatima" or "Eye of Fatima," in reference to Fatima Zahra, the daughter of Mohammad. Among the Jews, a fish is a symbol of good luck. This is why some hamsas have the fish included in the design, for extra luck and protection.

➢ **Healer's Hand:** This image is borrowed from Native American solar pictographs. In modern times, it is used to symbolize the healing Universal Energy released through the hands of a Reiki Practitioner or Spiritual Healer.

➢ **Hexagram:** A six-pointed star composed of two overlapped triangles, used by a number of faiths and cultures. It is known as the Star of David in the Jewish religion, but is also used in Hinduism, Buddhism, and Muslim regions. The hexagon is also called the "Seal of Solomon," and represents the Divine Union between female/male. It is composed of a downward pointing triangle representing the female energy and an upward pointing triangle representing the male energy. The traditional elemental triangles of Earth, Air, Water, and Fire are represented in this seal. It is also referred to as the "Star of Creation," the divine union of female and male, a symbol that opposites attract, and the universe is one.

Elemental triangles:

Air: △̵ *Fire:* △

Water: ▽ *Earth:* ▽̵

➢ **Hermetic Seal:** This symbol represents the body, mind, and spirit. In alchemy, it is used to represent Mercury, Salt, and Sulphur, and is a reference to the Philosopher's Stone—a legendary substance that was capable of turning inexpensive metals into gold. It is also used as an elixir of life in the hopes of achieving immortality (*See* J.K. Rowling's book *Harry Potter and the Philosopher's Stone*. Of course, there are many other books on this subject, but I actually read this one.)

➢ **Infinity:** It is the endless cycle of life. It is thought to be a mathematical symbol devised in the 1600s. In modern day, it is used with a more religious aspect referring to the never-ending cycle of life: birth, death, and re-birth. Similar symbols have been found in ancient Tibetan rock carvings, which are the Ouroboros, or infinity snake, drawn in this shape. In Tarot, it represents the balance of forces and is often associated with the Magician card.

Ouroboros

➢ **Kokopelli:** A Native American male fertility, trickster God that is represented as a humpbacked flute player who symbolizes the spirit of music. This figure of God Kokopelli comes from the ancient Anasazi (the Ancient Ones or Ancient Pueblo—cliff dwellers) glyphs. He is the God of Childbirth, as he is the one who carries unborn children on his back and distributes them to women. He often takes part in marriage rituals/ceremonies with a female consort, Goddess Kokopelmana. Kokopelli is the fertility God who presides over agriculture, his flute playing chases away the cold Winter in order for Spring to come in, and so that food is plentiful once again.

➢ **Labyrinth:** Labyrinth is a winding, maze-like path, often resembling a spiral. Labyrinths are found in many ancient cultures, and usually have spiritual significances. Labyrinths, in Medieval Times, were often in or on the floors of cathedrals, and were used as a sort of miniature pilgrimage. As the pilgrims walked the labyrinth path, they used this as a symbol of walking towards salvation or enlightenment. Labyrinths have seen a revival of sorts, as they are common in today's churches and Neo-Pagan sanctuaries.

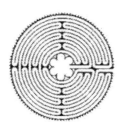

➤ **Lotus Flower:** The flower is sacred in Hindu, Buddhist, and Egyptian religions. The lotus is a water lily that rises from the murky waters to blossom as a symbol of purity of the soul within the material world, and an emblem of resurrection. The lotus is also a symbol that represents the seven chakras. As the leaves of the lotus unfold, your chakras unfold. As they become balanced, they expand your energies and awareness. The Buddhist use the lotus in their mandalas: an eight-petal lotus symbolizes cosmic harmony; a thousand-petal lotus symbolizes spiritual illumination; a bud symbolizes potential. A mandala (geometric art) is used for focusing one's attention, a spiritual teaching tool, to establish a sacred space, or as an aid for mediation.

➤ **Lunar Triple Goddess:** This symbol depicts the three phases of the moon: waxing crescent (maiden); full moon (mother); and waning crescent (crone); or the three stages of woman (maiden, mother, crone). The colors of the Lunar Triple Goddess symbol: maiden (waxing crescent) is the color white for birth and growth; mother (full moon) is the color red for life and love; and crone (waning crescent) is the color black for death and divination. This symbol is also used to represent the feminine polarity of the universe and the Triple Goddess.

➤ **Mudra:** This symbol represents Mudra, a spiritual gesture meaning peace, protection, power, or ridding one of fear and is used in the Buddhist and Hindu religions, and is similar to the christogram hand jester. This hand position is used during meditation.

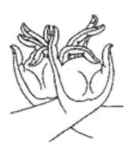

➤ **Om or Aum:** The primordial sound by which the earth was created. It is also referred to the "sound of the universe" or as the sound that is heard in outer space. Om is the original sound that contains all other sounds, all words, all languages, and all mantras. The Sanskrit name is *pranava,* meaning "to make a humming sound." It is placed at the beginnings and endings of most Hindu texts or to any prayer as a sacred exclamation.

➤ **Peace Sign:** This sign was adopted by the protestors of the Vietnam War (the 1960s anti-war movement), the flower children, and hippies, who made it their symbol as a show for peace, a non-violent show or cry for peace. Eventually, all Americans began using this as a sign for peace. The hand gesture regarding the peace symbol is the extension of the index finger and middle finger with the thumb holding down the bent ring finger and pinky, and holding the palm facing outwards.

➤ **Pentacle:** A pentacle is a pentagram within a circle that is used mostly by the Neo-Pagan faiths. The circle surrounding the five points is used to contain all the elements (Earth, Air, Fire, Water, and Spirit), their magical powers, and spiritual meanings in one place or space, where they are able to work as one, all for the greater good.

➢ **Scarab:** This is the symbol of Ra, the Sun God of the Egyptians. Scarab beetles lay their eggs in dung, which they roll into a ball and place in a hole. The dung is the food source for the Scarab beetles' larva. The Egyptians equated this with the movement of the Sun, its daily resurrection, and also associated it with reincarnation, or the cycle of life. The opening and closing of the scarab's colorful wings are said to symbolize night and day.

➢ **Skull and Crossbones:** The crossbones behind the skull is to warn of poison or danger. The crossbones under the skull (the Jolly Roger) indicate pirates or piracy. Also, skulls and crossbones are used in the entrances to cemeteries to denote a macabre, otherworldly realm. When used by the Freemasons or Masons, it is to symbolize a Master Mason. In today's use, it is more popular for tattoos, clothing, and jewelry.

➢ **Star of David:** The Biblical King David used this symbol—the Shield of David/Seal of Solomon during his flight from Saul. It was not associated specifically with the Jewish faith until the Middle Ages, when it became important to the Kabbalistics who are followers of the Kabbalah, the mystical part of Judaism. The hexagram symbolizes the six directions of space, the divine union of male and female energy, and the four elements.

Elemental triangles:

Air: *Fire:*

Water: *Earth:*

➢ **Triangle:** The upward pointing triangle, resembles a pyramid, is also the symbol of fire, male energy, a blade or phallus. The downward pointing triangle, resembling a chalice, is the symbol of water, female energy, the womb. The downward pointing triangle is one of the most ancient symbols for female divinity, as a representation of the genitalia of the Goddess. The triangle shape is also associated with the Christian Holy Trinity and the Masons.

➢ **Triple Horn of Odin:** The triple horn of the Norse God Odin is made of three interlocking horns. This symbol is also referred to as a "witch's claw." The horns are representative of the phallus, but they also represent a cup or challis and is associated with the feminine aspect of the Divine; the Triple Goddess.

➢ **Triquetra:** It symbolizes the Triple Goddess (maiden, mother, and crone). It is also considered to represent the following: mind, body, and soul; past, present, and future; Father, Son, and Holy Spirit. According to Celtic legend, it represents the three domains of the earth: land, sea, and sky.

➤ **Triskele or Triple Spiral:** It is composed of three interlocking spirals. The spiral is an ancient Celtic symbol used to refer to the sun—the never-ending cycle of life: birth, life, death, re-birth, or reincarnation. The Triple Spiral or Triskele is similar in meaning as the Triquetra.

➤ **Unicorn:** The symbol of the unicorn represents the male energy and power. This symbol was used in coats of arms, and in medieval tapestry art, it was a symbol to represent Christ.

➤ **Vitruvian Man:** This symbol is named after Vitruvius, an ancient Roman writer, architect, and engineer, who died in 15 B.C. This image or drawing by Leonardo da Vinci exemplifies the blend of art and science during the Renaissance period. Leonardo had an interest in proportions, and this was his attempt to relate man to nature. The square represents the material existence while the circle represents the spiritual existence. He made this as a study of the proportions of the (male) human body as described in writings by Vitruvius.

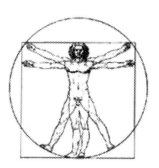

➤ **Yin-Yang:** Yin (moon) is passive, female, cold, and related to the left side of the human body. Yang (sun) is masculine, movement, heat, and related to the right side of the human body. The black side represents female/yin, while the white side represents the male/yang. It also shows that in order for humans to achieve balanced, we need to be in touch with both sides of ourselves—female/male, yin/yang.

> ➤ **Zia Sun Symbol:** The Zia Indians of New Mexico regard the Sun as a sacred symbol. This sacred symbol is used during celebrations to introduce newborns to the Sun, it is painted on ceremonial vases and drawn on the ground around campfires during celebrations honoring the Sun. Four is the sacred number of the Zia Indians. This emblem embodies the power of nature and man: the Sun, the four directions, the four seasons, and the four stages of life. This is also on the New Mexico State flag.

TELEPATHY

Telepathy is the communication of information via thoughts or feelings between humans; animals to humans; animals to animals; or humans to pets. This communication includes thoughts, ideas, feelings, sensations, and mental images. A telepath is one who has the ability to read the minds of others, human or animal.

THIRD EYE

The third eye, known as the "inner eye" or "mind's eye," is located between the two eyes, and is also the 6th Chakra. The color attributed to this Chakra is indigo or dark blue. Once opened, the third eye expands up to the middle of the forehead, and is considered one of the main energy centers of the body. The third eye is also part of the main meridian system of the body, which separates the two spheres; left and right.

The third eye symbolizes a state of enlightenment or higher consciousness. It is often associated with having visions, clairvoyance, precognition, or out-of-body experiences. People, who have developed the capacity to use their third eye, either innately or through meditation, are sometimes referred to as "seers."

In the Bible, Christ talks about the third eye: "If your eye is pure, there will be sunshine in your soul. However, if your eye is clouded with evil thoughts and desires, you are in deep spiritual darkness. And oh, how deep that darkness can be," Matthew 6:22-23. This sunshine or light in our soul is a reference to the Holy Spirit, as our eyes are windows to our spirit/soul or a representation of our enlightenment.

TRIPLE GODDESS

In ancient mythologies, many Goddesses would appear in threes (triad), either represented by three separate deities that would appear in a grouping or as a single Goddess portrayed in all three aspects as a Triple Goddess. The Celtic Goddess Morrigan who represented War, Fate, and Death, or the Greek Triple Goddess in the combination of Persephone—the maiden, pure, new beginnings, birth/re-birth; Demeter—the mother, full of life, giving, and compassionate; and Hecate—the crone, wise, all-knowing, and death. The Triple Goddess, seen as three-fold or as manifestations of different types of creativity, may perform different but related functions and may appear or represent any age (teen, 30-year-old, 70-year-old, etc.) that they desire for that particular function. The Triple Goddess also personifies the three phases of the moon: waxing crescent, full moon, and waning crescent. Symbols representing the Triple Goddess: Celtic Triskele and Lunar Triple Goddess

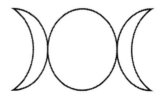

WINTER SOLSTICE
Also the time of Christmas, Yule, or Yuletide

The Winter Solstice occurs December 21 or December 22 and is referred to as the "shortest day and longest night" of the year. From this time forward, until the Summer Solstice, the days are getting longer. There are many holidays, festivals, rituals, and celebrations honoring re-birth or the return of the sun during this time of the year. December 25 is Christmas, the celebration of the birth of Christ. This was originally a pagan festival in pre-Christian times that honored the day the sun begins to return to the northern hemisphere. Yule celebrations coincide with Christmas celebrations, with such customs as decorating a fir or spruce tree (Christmas tree), burning a Yule log, hanging mistletoe and holly branches (garlands), giving gifts, eating ham, turkey, etc. The use of candles as decorations and as ritual items indicated the significance of honoring the deities of Light. The word "Yule" is a Scandinavian word, with "Yuletide" meaning the season of feasting. Yuletide is twelve days of feasting and partying, which begins twelve days prior to the Winter Solstice, and concludes on December 24. On December 25, fertility rites are performed referring to the Birthday of the Sun, the day the sun is re-born to stay longer in the sky each day. The twelve days of Christmas start the evening of December 24 through the morning of Epiphany, January 6. The Day of Epiphany is a Christian festival marking the visit of the Magi (the three wise men) to celebrate Christ's birth. The Day of Epiphany marks the beginning of the Mardi Gras season, which goes to Fat Tuesday, the day before Ash Wednesday, the beginning of Lent.

WISHING WELL

The term "wishing well" came from European folklore. Water was a source of life and often a scarce commodity, and it was thought that any spoken wish would be granted because water was thought to contain deities or is placed there by the Gods. The Celts considered springs and wells sacred places. People came to believe that these deities, guardians, or spirits of the wells would grant them their wish, but only if they paid a price. After uttering their wish and dropping the coin into the well, the wish would be granted based upon how the coin would land at the bottom of the well. If the coin is "heads-up," the wish would be granted, but if it is "heads-down," the wish would not be granted.

In Norse mythology, Mirmir, who is a giant and wisest of all beings and also the God of all the waters beneath the earth, guards the Well of Wisdom (also known as Mirmir's Well). He would grant infinite wisdom if one would sacrifice something that they held dear. The Norse God Odin, (who gave humanity Runes, which in today's time are used for divination), approached Mirmir for a drink of water from the well. Mirmir agreed, but only if Odin sacrificed an eye. Odin then had to suffer nine nights hanging upside-down on the world tree Yggdrasil. The Runes, the gift of knowledge and the ancient Norse alphabet, laid at the bottom of Mirmir's Well. With Odin, hanging upside-down on the world tree, groping blindly into the depths of the well, he was finally able to grasp the Runes and haul them forth for all humanity. The well is a symbol of the energies and resources that nourish the roots of all life (e.g., the world tree Yggdrasil or tree of life), and Odin delving into its depths, symbolized an inner process of reflection, a quest for truth and meaning.

Modern tradition, which stems from this, has us dropping pennies in ponds, fountains, and wells seeking that wish but not knowing we are leaving those small gifts to the deities as our thanks.

YIN-YANG

This is an ancient Chinese symbol representing how nature, humanity, the spirit world, the universe, etc. are all one or relate to each other. The outer circle represents how everything is held together, how they/we are all one. While the black (yin) and white (yang) shapes within the circle, represent the interaction of two energies, called "yin" (female/moon) and "yang" (male/sun).

The yin/yang symbol shows how these energies cannot exist without each other. Yin (female) is representative of the left side of the human body, with Yang (male) representative of the right side of the human body. Left-brain is female/yin; right-brain is male/yang.

While yin is dark, passive, downward, cold, contracting, and weak; yang is bright, active, upward, hot, expanding, and strong. If the male force (yang) is overwhelming, then there will be excessive heat (high temperature). If the female force (yin) is overwhelming, then there will be excessive cold (chills). The yin and yang symbol is in continual movement never ending, such as life itself or the universe.

If the spirit is hurt, and severe pain occurs first followed by swelling, it is thought there is a disagreement between the spirit and body, with the <u>spirit causing harm</u> to the body. If the body is hurt and swelling appears first followed by severe pain it is thought there is disharmony between the body and spirit, with the <u>body causing harm</u> to the spirit. When Yang is the controlling energy, a person can tolerate winter but not summer, but when Yin is the controlling energy, a person can tolerate summer but not winter. If a person is full of vigor and strength, then Yin and Yang are in proper harmony.

REFERENCES

While researching for my book, I referred to www.wikipedia.org and www.about.com often.

Animal Totems:
http://www.mystical-www.co.uk/animal/ania2z.htm or http://www.starstuffs. com and *Animal-Wise* by Ted Andrews.

Color:
http://www.angelfire.com/tx/wiccanfeatherwood/colors.html.

Crystals and Gemstones: *The Crystal Bible* by Judy Hall.

Divination:
http://www.answers.com/topic/divination and http://skepdic.com/divinati.html.

Ear Candling:
http://healing.about.com/od/earcandling/Ear_Candling.htm

Feng Shui:
http://www. fengshui-tips. com/;
http://www.fengshuibasics.com/plants.htm; and
http://www.ganeshaspeaks.com/blog_Tips_to_Energize_your_Home_with_the_power_of_plants_and_flowers_1159.jsp; and.

Sanskrit:
http://www.swargarohan.org/Glossary.htm;
http://learn-sanskrit.com/sanwords.htm
http://www.hinduwebsite.com/hinduism/h_meaning.asp.

Symbols:
http://en.wikipedia.org/wiki/List_of_symbols

Yin/Yang:
http://fly.cc.fer.hr/~shlede/ying/yang.html

Index

Brenda Miller lives in Austin, Texas with her daughter, Mikayla. She has worked in the legal field as a corrections officer and legal secretary/legal assistant for over 25 years. At the age of 50, she is starting the second half of her existence here on Mother Earth in a new direction, seeking a more spiritual, peaceful stress-free life.

MISCELLANEOUS

Front cover and back cover artwork by Brenda Miller. Ogham and Rune illustrations by Brenda Miller. The symbol that is on the front cover is called Johre Calligraphy—White Light. The White Light give off a vibrancy of 2,520 electrons that when run through a prism refracts into the seven primary colors, e.g. colors of the chakras. It is used in spiritual healing modalities such as Reiki.